Depression

THE COMMONSENSE APPROACH

The CommonSense Approach Series

This series of self-help guides from Newleaf provides practical and sound ways to deal with many of life's common complaints.

Each book in the series is written for the layperson, and adopts a commonsense approach to the many questions surrounding a particular topic. It explains what the complaint is, how and why it occurs, and what can be done about it. It includes advice on helping ourselves, and information on where to go for further help. It encourages us to take responsibility for our own health, to be sensible and not always to rely on medical intervention for every ill.

AVAILABLE IN THIS SERIES

Addiction — The CommonSense Approach	Michael Hardiman
Headaches — The CommonSense Approach	Pat Thomas
Menopause — The CommonSense Approach	Ruth Appleby
Men's Health — The CommonSense Approach	Joe Armstrong
Pregnancy — The CommonSense Approach	Pat Thomas
Sleep — The CommonSense Approach	Brenda O'Hanlon
Stress — The CommonSense Approach	Brenda O'Hanlon

Depression

THE COMMONSENSE APPROACH

Tony Bates

Newleaf

Newleaf
an imprint of
Gill & Macmillan Ltd
Hume Avenue, Park West
Dublin 12
with associated companies throughout the world
www.gillmacmillan.ie

ISBN-13: 978 07171 2860 0

Index compiled by Helen Litton
Design by Identikit Design Consultants, Dublin
Print origination by Carole Lynch
Printed by ColourBooks Ltd, Dublin

This book is typeset in Revivial565 9.5pt on 15pt.

The paper used in this book comes from the wood pulp of managed forests. For every tree felled, at least one tree is planted, thereby renewing natural resources.

A catalogue record for this book is available from the British Library.

16 15

Contents

While the author has made every effort to ensure that the information contained in this book is accurate, it should not be regarded as an alternative to professional medical advice. Readers should consult their general practitioners or physicians if they are concerned about aspects of their own health, and before embarking on any course of treatment. Neither the author nor the publishers can accept responsibility for any health problem resulting from using, or discontinuing, any of the drugs described here, or the self-help methods described.

Foreword

Depression haunts the lives of many and is more and more common in the Western world. This is particularly so for women. There are many explanations for why this might be, including increasing role strain for women, fragmentation of communities, changing expectations, and feelings of needing to compete with others to prove oneself worthy, competent and able. Whatever the sources, Dr Bates has written a useful book which helps potential sufferers understand the nature of depression, what it feels like to be depressed and more importantly that depression is an eminently treatable condition. Once one is able to recognise and be honest with oneself about the nature of depression then there are various things that can be done.

Different people with different types of depression benefit from different types of treatment. Some people gain enormous benefit from medication which returns their sleep to reasonable levels, reduces anxiety to within tolerable limits and helps them dwell less on the negatives in their lives. Depression can be a state of exhaustion when people become physically and psychologically exhausted and those around them can feel the same. Medication can help energy levels return. However, many people want to go beyond this and to try to understand how they became depressed and more importantly what they can do to help themselves. Dr Bates has written clearly on this subject. He describes how people's depressions are often (but by no means always) rooted in deep fears and concerns about the adequacy or inadequacy of oneself. Underlying feelings of worthlessness, inferiority and failure which may have been gained in childhood can resurface again and again in times of life crisis. This makes the crisis and the stress in our lives more difficult to cope with than need be because we continually see it through the lens of it indicating our own personal failures once again. This book outlines how commonly this occurs for people who suffer depression, and discusses what one can do to identify those typical depression thoughts and how one can begin to challenge them.

Dr Bates shares with us a number of his own experiences in treating depressed patients and highlights some of the key things that have helped those people. From these kinds of self-help books one hopes for two things. Firstly, that depression can be seen as a sadness, sometimes a tragedy but never a shame. With over one hundred million depressed people in the world today we have to see depression as a disorder which has an origin, a course and a treatment. Depression is no respecter of status, intelligence, class or race. It can strike anyone at any time. It is related to various interacting forces in our current lives, in our past lives and in our bodies. The more we are able to confront depression honestly and without shame, the better position we will be in to help ourselves recover. Dr Bates has outlined a programme which not only helps to de-shame the experiences of depression but points to some key processes that can aid recovery.

Professor Paul Gilbert F.B.Ps.S.
Mental Health Research Unit, Derby

Acknowledgments

My thanks to my wife, Ursula, Professor Marcus Webb and my editor, Eveleen Coyle, for their support in allowing me see this work through to its completion. Particular thanks to Deirdre McHugh for her sensitive critique of several drafts. To those individuals whose stories are relayed in disguised form, and to all who cannot be named, my sincere thanks. Their struggle has given me the hope for recovery contained in these pages. My thanks also to Michael-Paul Gallagher, S.J., Eamonn Butler and Professor Paul Gilbert, for their encouragement and patience in reviewing drafts of this work. I dedicate this book to the late Therese Brady, psychologist, mentor and friend, who never lost sight of the dignity of each person in the midst of their pain, and who taught me to balance compassion for suffering with a respect for the resilience and strength that lies in the heart of every human being.

I would like to say to anybody that feels like I felt, that there is hope. You are as good as anybody else and the only one you have to prove that to is yourself. So get whatever help you need now. Don't wait until you're forty-three years old like I did. Because you know the feeling long before that.

Francis, 1993

Introduction

Depression is a thief that steals from people; it robs them of energy, vitality, self-esteem, and any pleasure that they might previously have enjoyed. For some the physical intensity of their pain and despair makes suicide appear the only possible solution. Depression makes one self-centred but not selfish. As with a throbbing toothache, it's hard to think about anything except your own personal hell when you are depressed.

Depression can have a very destructive impact on families and loved ones. Children cannot but sense and feel troubled by a parent's dark moods, partners even more so. The effort to alleviate the pain of depression in a loved one inevitably fails and even the most well-intended interventions of friends and spouses can leave all concerned feeling helpless and alienated. Depression can create havoc in the lives of all it touches and sow seeds of misunderstanding and anger that persist long after the gloom has lifted. While this book is primarily intended as a guide to recovery for the sufferer, it is also written with relatives and friends of the sufferer in mind, in the hope that it may make sense of what can be a difficult problem to grasp from the 'outside'. Understanding of the problem by all who are affected can act as a bridge between those who feel isolated and those who feel alienated by depression.

Susan was tall, blonde and in her late twenties. Her outward appearance suggested a self-contained, confident woman, but her eyes told a different story. She looked as if she'd rather have been anywhere but my office the day she first arrived. Her movements were awkward and stiff. Eye contact was avoided and I hesitated to ask her why she'd come, sensing it might be an invasion of a privacy which was being anxiously guarded. We danced around the central issue for a while as I pieced together a profile of her family background, her schooling and occupation, and her current circumstances. She relaxed a little but when I asked what had brought her to see me, her fragile holding together gave way to a flood of tears.

Words failed Susan as she tried vainly to account for her terrible sadness. She felt she had no right to complain but she described how in recent weeks she had found herself collapsing into tears for no apparent reason, overcome by the feeling that she was stupid, worthless and completely out of control. She apologised repeatedly for her demeanour. She struck me as someone who didn't normally, if ever, let down her guard about her inner struggles. But on this occasion the intensity of her inner pain refused to be silenced and she had sought counselling to help her make some sense of it all.

In writing this book, I think about Susan on that first visit, and many others who have come and confronted the intense inner pain that is depression. All have been confused and frightened by what was happening to them. Their own desperation, the experience of 'losing a grip' on work and life, or the helpless exasperation of close loved ones, prompted them to reach out and look for help. I imagine you are reading this book having struggled also with depression, perhaps directly, or indirectly through living with someone who is visited and revisited by this problem. My hope is that you will find in Susan's story, and in the account of others' struggles with depression, some echo of your own experience. Also that you will discover that you are not 'mad' or 'stupid' or 'horribly selfish'. There are reasons why someone becomes depressed; being able to understand and make sense of the experience restores morale.

In this book we will consider some strategies for moving out of depression and these will be mostly straightforward and practical. However, there is another theme that will run through these pages and hopefully make sense to you: if depression distorts my sense of who I am, how do I recover a sense of my true self? Maybe you've never been very clear about who you are.

One of the advantages of struggling with depression is that you take up a quest to get to know and express your true self.

As we travel together through these pages, you may want to consider that you are not what your present negative mood says you are: you are not the 'stupid', 'inadequate', 'hopeless' or 'unlovable' person that you believe you are right now. You're a human being, no better or no worse than others whom you admire. You're as unique and as interesting as they are and equally deserving of respect and encouragement. Don't expect to feel convinced of this at the moment, but even your choosing to read this book suggests that somewhere inside, you believe that you deserve more. This book will speak to that part of you that wants more out of life, that inner voice that refuses to give in to depression. It may only be a tiny voice at the moment, but my aim in these pages is to strengthen that voice and help you discover a truer, healthier sense of who you really are. Someone who includes and makes room for personal vulnerability, but who never loses sight of their capacity for joy. Someone you'd be glad to wake up to each morning.

How can we even aspire to achieve something so important in a short book such as this? Let me say this first so neither of us has any illusions: nobody can magically take away depression. I can only join with someone who is in this particular pain and help them to discover a strength in themselves to fight it. You will need to struggle and do battle with your inner demons of shame, self-criticism and self-loathing on which depression feeds. You may be drowning under the weight of all this now and you need a solid ally to help you fight your way back. As allies go I'm not the worst. I've worked with depressed people for over twenty years and battled through my own dark night of the soul. Like a tracker who has been in and out of the jungle many times, I can serve as a guide to help you plot your course and prevent you from going round in circles, retracing your steps through the same waste ground over and over.

Sarah's Recovery Journal

Excerpt 1

Depression is like an assignment in life that nobody ever sets for you to do. No one tells you beforehand how difficult it's going to be, how time-consuming it is, how painful it can be. You're not prepared for it and when it happens you want to give it all away and collapse into nothing. Because there are no real signs, no real markers, no sheets handed out beforehand telling you what it's going to be like. And before you know it you're being judged, not on your progress but on your failures, on your weaknesses. The judge isn't a fair one with guidelines and suggestions. The judge is yourself, the 'worst' around, who shatters your confidence and who plays on your vulnerabilities until you get to the point where you want to break. You want to give up on this assignment which seems so wasteful and pointless. But it's really the most important assignment you'll be given. It's an essay which is long and tiresome but where you must come out with full marks. Those full marks won't be given for content or structure or quality. They'll be given each time you believe in yourself and care for yourself a little more. And you're the one who calls out the grade, because you're the one giving yourself those stars. The assignment is you, and you are the judge, the expert, the one who knows you and cares about you and loves you enough to say, 'I'm worth it, I'm worth 100 per cent.'

I've tried to combine the best advice from scientific research with the most practical tips learned from the people I've helped. Ultimately, it is these people who have taught me the most, and provided critical insights from their struggle with depression.

One of the stories which is revisited throughout this book is that of 'Sarah', a twenty-year-old woman who struggled successfully with a severe depression for twelve months. During all that time she kept a journal. With her permission, key excerpts have been selected to illustrate the issues addressed in each of the following chapters. The first excerpt above was written towards the end of her recovery.

There is much more that could be said about this problem than any one book could cover. This book is no substitute for you finding a trustworthy professional to work with you in your recovery. Self-help literature is often most useful when it is employed as an adjunct to personal therapy. We will talk more about this later, but do consider that there is a time for recruiting some one-to-one specialist help in the fight against depression. Finding the right person may take time but one of the benefits of reading this book may be that it will clarify what you may need from a professional in your particular struggle to overcome depression.

CHAPTER 1

Recognising Depression

◆◆◆

Depression! Depression is not a word that for a long time I would have applied to myself. In retrospect, however, I would probably now accept that I have been depressed over a long number of years and in need of some help.

◆◆◆

We have all been 'a bit depressed' on occasions. We often use this phrase to describe how we feel when life gets too much for us. Yet it rarely implies that we are suffering from depression in the sense that it is meant in this book. It is important to distinguish those times when it is normal and expected that one might feel sad from those times when we are caught in the grip of what is termed 'clinical depression'.

The everyday use of the term 'depression' more often refers to what can happen when we are dealing with some stressful or challenging event in our lives that wears us down. Relationships at home or at work that are full of conflict can contribute to this sense of 'life being too much'. It may be that we are understandably sad, even shattered, by the loss of someone we loved. There is a period of feeling very low that inevitably comes in the wake of such a loss which reflects just how much that individual meant to us. A time of mourning is very important in that it allows us to acknowledge the absence of a loved one and adjust gradually to living our lives without them. While this can be a heartbreaking time, a person can endure and survive it with loving support. After the period of acute mourning has passed they can feel stronger in themselves and appreciate how their lives have been both saddened and deepened by their grief.

Clinical depression is not just about feeling sad, bereaved or overstressed. It is characterised by a persistent low mood, a lack of energy, difficulty with concentration and memory, and a striking lack of interest in things that are normally a source of pleasure and stimulation. Unlike the experience of being sad or upset, depression doesn't respond readily to the concerns of others, some pleasant distraction, or some novel or joyful event. It holds the sufferer hostage and seems to refuse to consider all reasonable offers to set them free. Depression generally provokes a withdrawal from others and a turning against oneself. The sufferer is left with the conviction that they have not merely suffered some setback or important loss, but that they themselves are 'losers', and that nothing will ever be resolved in their life.

Sarah's Recovery Journal

Excerpt 2

These days I don't know what to do with my time. Almost everything seems so futile, nothing seems to have any importance any more. I don't feel really depressed all the time just bogged down with living. I spend a lot of time in a daze, as though I'm hiding things from myself; my memory is blocked, my feelings are blocked and I feel like a walking stone statue. Some of the time I think I feel OK, but then my mood changes and I become frightened again. I move back on occasions during the day to those so familiar periods of despair when inside my head I can hear myself screaming, 'Help me, what am I supposed to do?'

In the early stage of her depression Sarah described her experience in her journal. Her account conveys the sense of confusion and isolation so characteristic of depression.

Depression is characterised by a particular set of changes in the way a person thinks, feels and behaves. As well as being an experience of psychological suffering it reduces a person's sense of physical well-being and affects their sleep, appetite and level of energy. The primary symptoms of depression are discussed below and illustrated in the following diagram. Symptoms generally are grouped according to how they impact on our thinking, feelings, behaviours and physical state. Each group of symptoms impacts on the others, drawing the individual deeper into a negative mental and physical state.

SYMPTOMS OF DEPRESSION

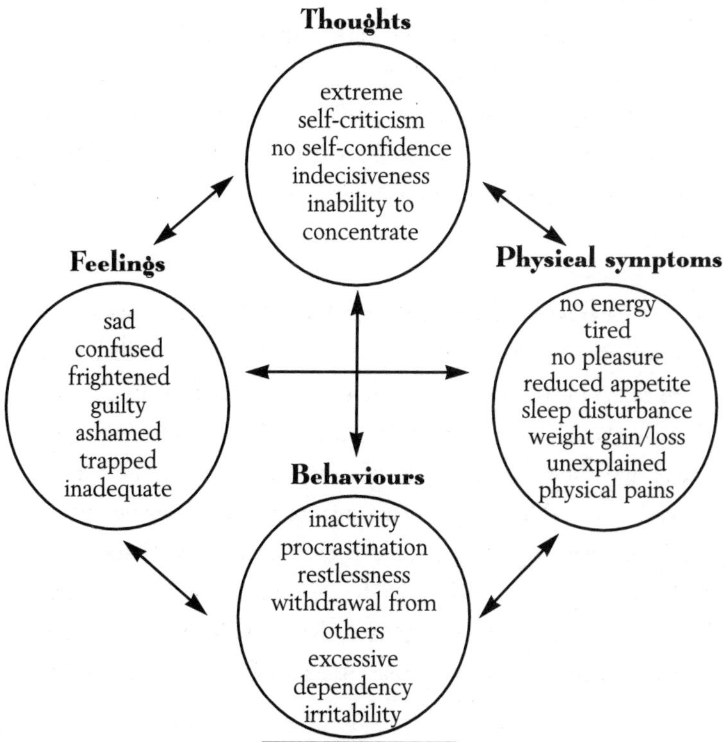

Thinking Characteristic of Depression

A depressed individual's thinking is characterised by extreme self-criticism, pessimism, hopelessness about the future, and a profound conviction that they are in some way a failure as a human being. For depressed people important achievements in their past no longer seem to count as they focus exclusively on every sign of failure or weakness that they can possibly point to in their life. These preoccupations seriously reduce their ability to concentrate — a very depressed person may find it hard to read more than a paragraph of a newspaper or book. Such is their loss of confidence that even the simplest decisions they are faced with can prove to be an enormous strain: they cannot trust themselves to do the right thing.

Perhaps the most common presentation of depression is where the individual experiences obsessive negative thinking from which he or she can't distract themselves. These individuals are constantly troubled because they experience themselves as being out of control and helpless in terms of managing their lives. Living each day feels frightening and unpredictable. They dread that something bad could happen because they feel that they have no reserves to cope with any further stress in their lives.

Feelings Characteristic of Depression

A depressed person may be in such intense distress that they are reluctant to discuss their inner turmoil for fear others may be shocked. They feel incapable of describing exactly how they feel and they may be confused and frightened by their inner experiences. The fear of being misunderstood or criticised by others encourages them to keep their feelings to themselves. These feelings typically include feelings of shame, guilt and anxiety. For the depressed person there is very little in life that gives pleasure. Activities that previously were important to them no longer hold their interest. Themes of sadness or gloom may permeate their conversation. Sarah described the feeling of being depressed in the following way:

> I'm so distressed because I don't know what's going on in my head. It's confusing and I feel frightened and unsure about everything I do. I used to be happy and cheerful and confident. I used to enjoy my life. Where is everything gone? I don't understand why I feel like this, why I feel so worn out, sad and lonely. I need warmth. I need to be warmed up inside. Everything's gone cold and strange. I'd love for someone to give me a big hug, but if I asked I feel that they wouldn't understand why and that they would think I was crazy.

Physical Symptoms Characteristic of Depression

Depression is for many people a very physical experience and the symptoms they describe are often to do with changes they experience in their body. They may describe the sensation of hurting deeply inside or they may have vague physical symptoms which worry them, but which have no apparent physical cause. Sleep disturbance is probably the most common physical symptom of depression. Sufferers usually report a broken sleep pattern that results in waking early without the sense of being rested or refreshed. Their normal appetite is also affected, resulting in either excessive eating and weight gain, or a complete lack of interest in food, which leads to increasing weight loss. They may also find themselves unable to make love and indeed have very little interest in doing so, and this can be a major worry for them.

Behaviour Characteristic of Depression

In adults and children alike depression can go unnoticed for long periods as they express the problem in unexpected ways. For example, an adolescent may begin to act in an uncharacteristic way, participating in shoplifting, fire-setting or disruptive behaviour at school. An adult may complain of a problem of sexual impotence, severe procrastination, or vague physical complaints for which there is no apparent cause. Often adults abuse alcohol to kill the pain, which makes them feel worse in the long run, and compounds their basic sense of inadequacy. Alcohol can dull the pain of depression temporarily, but it is a drug which actually intensifies the sufferer's mood when taken to excess.

A significant slowing down in activity is a very common feature of depression although some sufferers can become restless, even hyperactive, as they try to block out the sense of torment they experience inside. Excessive 'busy-ness' can be a protective mechanism to distract us when we are in turmoil, but it leaves us feeling constantly on edge and irritable, especially with close loved ones who are more likely to notice something is wrong. It seems preferable to the prospect of slowing down and acknowledging that something is not right. Susan, whom we mentioned in the introduction, put this very succinctly when she said, 'You make yourself very vulnerable when you stop to think!'

Most commonly, the depressed person's behaviour is marked by lethargy, lack of energy and procrastination. One man, who was in his mid-thirties, described how his 'get-up-and-go was all gone'. There is little energy to devote to external demands and concerns. A tendency to take to the bed is all too common. The experience of depression makes one feel very isolated, whether or not there are others around, and sometimes it can seem easier just to retreat into one's own company to avoid having to deal with the criticism, demands, even concerns, of loved ones and friends.

Different Types of Depression

Depression varies in terms of how severely it affects each person: it may be experienced to a mild, moderate or severe degree. In its mild or moderate forms, it is characterised by negative thinking and low self-esteem, irritability, and difficulty in concentrating. If this state of mind continues over an extended period of time (at least one year) the individual is deemed to be suffering from what is termed 'Dysthymia', which is like a low-grade form of depression that endures for a long period, and can easily go unnoticed. In the more severe forms of depression the same symptoms are experienced with greater intensity and there are also physical manifestations of this mental torment. Symptoms of fatigue, insomnia or hypersomnia (too little or too much sleep), decreased appetite, significant change in weight and a marked slowing down of physical and mental activity, indicate the need for specialised help. Suicidal thoughts often lurk just beneath the surface and should always be checked for and regarded with the utmost seriousness. A diagnosis of severe or 'Major Depression' is applicable if the majority of these symptoms are experienced every day for at least *two weeks*.

'Bipolar' or 'Manic Depression' refers to severe episodes of depression which are interspersed with at least one episode of elation or mania. A pattern of mood swings is observable over time, where the above symptoms of major depression can alternate with the individual experiencing extreme agitation and elation. During these 'high' episodes, the sufferer may exhibit pressured speech, inappropriate behaviour that is out of character for them, and sometimes beliefs that are compelling for the sufferer, but entirely irrational.

Recognising Depression in Children and Adolescents

There has been increasing attention to the growing incidence of depression in childhood and adolescence. The same criteria which we used above to diagnose depression have been found to apply to children but with certain modifications. For example, studies find that four out of five depressed children are more likely to strike one as irritable rather than sad. Children also tend to externalise their suffering in the form of disruptive behaviour which can result in them being perceived as having 'conduct disorders'. The experience of depression with which they are trying to struggle can often be overlooked.

Some researchers have found that depressed children, especially pre-schoolers and pre-adolescents, are unlikely to report feeling sad and hopeless but instead can tend to 'look' depressed in both their facial expression and their posture. When children reach the age of adolescence their depressed mood is similar to that of adults. They will report feeling depressed and often complain of physical or somatic symptoms which bother them. With older teenagers depression is likely to coexist with eating disorders and substance abuse disorders. Other symptoms that are noted are social withdrawal, excessive worrying and conduct problems.

Suicidal thoughts and attempts are quite common in depressed young people, occurring in two-thirds of depressed pre-schoolers, pre-adolescents and adolescents. Studies have reported actual suicide attempts in 6 to 12 per cent of depressed children and young adolescents. These rates appear to be higher among youths than among depressed adults.

Post-partum Depression

Many women can exhibit symptoms after childbirth that include crying, insomnia, poor appetite. These experiences are considered normal responses to the profound shifts in hormones experienced at such a time. However, when a major depressive episode develops a few weeks after delivery it may be identified as a post-partum depression. The symptoms of this disorder are similar to those of clinical depression. These women have often been found to have had emotional problems and vulnerabilities prior to giving birth. In a small percentage of women who experience this disorder the symptoms that develop can be extremely severe and crippling. Some women who dearly looked forward to giving birth to their child seem to turn against the child in a way that is completely out of character for them. They may become convinced that the child is 'bad' in some way and act in ways that neglect the child or even endanger its life. This vulnerability to severe post-partum depression is particularly noted among women who have histories of Bipolar depression. Obviously, women who experience these latter symptoms are in urgent need of medical attention both for their own protection and that of the child. Hospital admission is very frequently recommended for severe post-partum depression even though it has the adverse effect of separating mother and child at a very critical time of their bonding. Hard decisions often have to be made by family and health care staff and ultimately the decision may be to give priority to the woman's recovery and trust that this will also be in the best interest of the child.

Who Gets Depressed?

The prevalence of depression in the general population is reported to be on average 5.2 per cent at any given time. This is accepted to be an underestimate rather than a true figure. Mostly, it occurs in individuals aged between twenty-five and sixty-five years, with the incidence increasing with age. Estimates for the over-sixty-five group are that between 10 and 17 per cent are significantly depressed at any one time. In spite of its frequency — depression has been called the *common cold of psychiatry* — only one in ten of the people who become depressed seek help professionally. Unfortunately, many sufferers do not seek help of any kind due to a feeling of shame about what they regard as a flaw in their character.

Though the great majority of cases occur in adults, depression may occur at any time from early childhood to old age. One study of 3,000 schoolchildren found that 5 per cent of the group were reporting mild to moderate depression. Chronic marital conflict, parental rejection, or serious stresses in adjusting to school more often account for such reactions in children. Sadness, anxiety and fearfulness may characterise childhood depression, but this problem is often reflected in poor school work and aggressive behaviour which may mislead parents into thinking these children are simply misbehaving.

One remarkably consistent finding in studies across different continents has been that women are about twice as likely to experience depression as men. The greatest number of depressed women are in the twenty to forty age group. However, men and women become depressed in equal numbers where they are in similar roles such as in student life or in professional careers. Whether or not women's biological constitution renders them more likely to become depressed than men has been hotly debated. Women are no more vulnerable to depression than men when they are not dealing with added stresses of home and family coupled with isolation and lack of social support.

Measuring Your Own Mood

What have you learned from the above? Do you recognise something of your own experience of depression? Perhaps you have been afraid to acknowledge that something was wrong and yet it's becoming easier now for you to name it — to put a face on the enemy. To help you clarify what your experience of depression has been, review the checklist below of the twelve most common symptoms of depression, based on the diagnostic criteria of the American Psychiatry Association. Read each symptom and tick yes to any that describe how you have been feeling, most of the time, over at least the past two weeks. We are all prone to having any of these symptoms on a 'bad day', but what characterises clinical depression is that these symptoms are experienced persistently for at least a *two-week* period.

DEPRESSION CHECKLIST

Indicate which of these symptoms you've experienced over the past two weeks by ticking yes or no:

	YES	NO
1. I have been feeling down most of the time.	___	___
2. I get no pleasure from the things that normally mean a lot to me.	___	___
3. I feel tired all the time.	___	___
4. I can't concentrate and remember details.	___	___
5. I have lost weight quite dramatically.	___	___
6. My sleep is disturbed and doesn't leave me feeling rested.	___	___
7. I am more irritable than usual.	___	___
8. I have lost all confidence in my ability to make decisions.	___	___
9. My thoughts are mostly self-critical and gloomy.	___	___
10. I feel guilty without really knowing why.	___	___
11. I feel sensations in my body that trouble me.	___	___
12. I have thoughts of killing myself.	___	___

If you have ticked 'Yes' to either of the first two items and 'Yes' to at least four of the remaining items, this suggests that you may be experiencing a treatable depression. The higher your score the more severe your depression.

Pay particular attention to your answer for the last item on the checklist, question 12, which concerns suicidal thoughts. While it's common for depressed people to think that everything would be somehow easier if they were dead, it's important to emphasise that if these thoughts are more than just occasional or if they have progressed to where you are actively thinking about ways to 'end it all', then it is imperative that you seek some professional help.

Summary

Depression has some universal characteristics but each individual experiences slightly different combinations of symptoms. For some it's an intensely physical experience and affects their energy level and overall sense of well-being. Others can somehow keep going but their hyperactivity is based on running away. Some sufferers are prone to long spells of inner torment as they are overwhelmed by negative thoughts and feelings of tremendous personal failure. If this distress continues over a long period their ability to function is inevitably compromised. Personal relationships can become severely strained, and work colleagues may notice them being edgy, falling behind, procrastinating on important projects, or withdrawing from the company of others. However it is sparked, depression confuses and frightens the sufferer and it becomes an extremely isolating and lonely experience.

CHAPTER 2

What Causes Depression?

Most depressions are best understood as an end product of stress impacting on specific vulnerabilities in an individual's personality and social circumstances. Negative early life experiences, rigid rules for living, stressful social pressures and biological vulnerabilities can render a person prone to depression and these are discussed separately below.

Early Childhood Experiences that Leave us Prone to Depression

Perhaps the most striking characteristic of depression-prone individuals is their belief that there is something fundamentally bad or incompetent about them as human beings. This is often referred to as having a poor self-image. The image we have of ourselves is principally formed through the feedback we receive from those most closely involved in our rearing. An unresponsive parent or a constantly critical or abusive parent will eventually create within the child a sense that they are not adequate or loved.

Traumas such as the loss of a parent, severe illness and hospitalisation can also undermine a child's sense of security. Numerous studies have tested a theory that depression is caused by loss of a parent in early childhood which in turn creates a vulnerability to becoming depressed later in life. Similar experiences in adult life, or the threat of loss or abandonment by a loved one, can awaken these painful memories which have never been resolved, and which are often buried subconsciously. This finding has been borne out in many studies but most recent research has found that what is most critical is the care that a child experiences following the early loss. Thus, parental loss followed by lack of consistent care for the child does seem to be predictive of later depression.

Studies of depressed children and adolescents reveal that these individuals did not feel they had a close relationship with their parents. These sufferers describe their mothers and fathers as rejecting, controlling, and as showing very little warmth. The conclusion from research is that child-rearing styles that are marked by 'low affection' and 'high control' are consistently related to depression. Parents who set high standards, and who are harshly critical, intrusive and controlling in an attempt to get their children to meet their high expectations, produce children who constantly berate themselves and attack themselves as worthless.

The quality of the attachment bond between child and parent appears to set the stage for depression. Very often the harshness that permeates a parent's way of relating to their children directly reflects the lack of affection they themselves received as children. As a result of their own difficult upbringing they cannot respond comfortably to their own children's emotional needs and they discourage affection-seeking or dependent behaviour. Children exposed to such experiences may become depressed, while adults who experience such events in childhood may be vulnerable to depressive reaction when faced with similar experiences in later life. These influences seem to work by creating in the mind of the person negative thoughts about their own worth and competence as individuals. Poor early relationships also impair the individual's capacity to form healthy relationships which could help them avoid or resolve stressful situations.

Rigid Rules of Living

Coping strategies are worked out on the basis of many recurrent experiences in our early life and they eventually become laid down in our minds as rules for living. We each come to a personal conclusion about what we need to do in order to achieve some sense of belonging and to feel good about ourselves. When these rules are framed rigidly in our minds we remain very vulnerable to becoming depressed when something happens that breaks the rules, or when we are simply unable to live by them.

For example, those who were hurt by an unresponsive or harshly critical parent may devote a lot of energy to making sure they are liked and approved of by others. They live by the coping strategy, or 'rule', that says 'To feel good about myself, I must make sure I'm liked by other people' or 'In order to be accepted and loved, I must always put others' needs first.' They subordinate their own needs and wishes in favour of serving others' needs. They satisfy themselves with what acceptance this earns them in the eyes of others and they suppress their own individuality.

Other people cope by adopting a rule of living which says that 'To feel good about myself I must perform perfectly and always be on top of things.' They measure their worth exclusively in terms of achievement and their ability to 'go it alone'. They believe their achievements gain them significant respect and they fear any kind of failure which they believe will diminish them in the eyes of others. Their childhood experience convinces them that no matter how much they yearn to be close, it is not safe to do so. They live a life based on the belief that they must rely on themselves alone as other people cannot be relied upon, and they themselves are lacking whatever it is that might make others want to support them. Underlying these coping strategies there remains a desire to feel close and to belong. The frustration of this need leaves them vulnerable to depression. The experience of feeling excluded from intimate relationships and unable to achieve a sense of belonging is a deep loss which can easily turn into depression.

While these rules are genuine attempts to maintain some degree of self-esteem and protect oneself from the deep suspicion that one is bad or unlovable, they can leave a person very vulnerable to depression. To build one's self-confidence on the shifting sands of other people's approval is clearly a very dubious and dangerous venture. Inevitably, there will be conflict in relationships and some people are bound to disapprove of what we do no matter how careful we are not to offend them. People with an excessive need for approval remain constantly vulnerable to feeling bad about themselves when they encounter opposition or disapproval.

Clinical experience suggests that the self-loathing and self-criticism so common in depression sufferers often reflects the attitude taken towards them as children. However, for some sufferers these negative thinking patterns are an overstatement of what they have been exposed to in early life. Their negative thoughts become activated by some event that seems to signal that they are not acceptable/lovable, and thereafter their self-esteem spirals downward. Everywhere they look they seem to find confirmation that their worst fears about themselves are true. Depression distorts perception in such a way that even positive events become twisted in the mind of the sufferer, and are interpreted as proof that there is something bad about oneself. Thus a genuine compliment given quite spontaneously to the individual can be interpreted along the lines: 'God, I must look so pathetic that someone felt they had to say something to cheer me up.'

Social Circumstances

There are factors that can directly undermine a person's self-esteem which have to do with their current social situation. Poor housing, social isolation and the pressures of rearing young children with no support increase vulnerability to depression. One interesting piece of research which highlights the crucial role of social support in staying mentally well is the finding that women in stressful social circumstances with even one close, confiding friend were four times less likely to become depressed than those women in similar circumstances who did not have such a friendship. We all need friendship to lighten the burdens we carry, to restore our trust in ourselves when we lose it, and to break the grip of loneliness that can so easily overtake us when we become depressed.

Our self-esteem derives partly from what we do and from the feeling that we are making some valued contribution to others. Regular employment gives us a measure of control over our lives, and offers numerous opportunities for satisfying interaction with others. Unemployment therefore clearly has an impact on an individual's self-esteem and where there is any vulnerability to depression it undoubtedly aggravates it. Research has found that being employed decreases one's chance of becoming depressed by a factor of ten; in other words, individuals in difficult social situations are ten times more likely to be depressed if they are without employment than if they do have steady employment.

Many different forms of social injustice exist that can erode an individual's sense of dignity. The experience of repeatedly trying, in vain, to rectify a bad situation can eventually produce in them a condition psychologists call 'learned helplessness'. This is a state of mind that develops where one believes that nothing one does matters since control over one's life is totally in the hands of others. People in such situations find that stresses gradually build up which never seem to get resolved until something finally happens that is simply 'the last straw', which breaks their spirit and throws them into depression. Bullying in any form over a period of time is one form of injustice that can produce depression.

Biological Factors

Specific biological vulnerabilities have been suggested to explain those recurrent depressions that have a striking physical component. In these conditions movement and speech can be slow, and the sufferer wakes early and feels unable to face the day, but finds that their mood seems to lift as the day goes on. Appetite is diminished and weight loss may become quite noticeable.

This biological explanation of depression believes that there are specific biochemical changes in the brain that affect our mood. Research is not clear what exactly these changes are, but attention has been focused particularly on the role of three chemicals which are involved with regulating our emotions. These are dopamine, noradrenaline and serotonin. Antidepressants work by increasing the availability of these chemicals in the brain. Serotonin is a neurotransmitter which has received particular attention of late. In severe episodes of depression there is believed to be a reduction in the amount of serotonin available in the brain which in turn causes fatigue, listlessness and sleep disturbance so characteristic of depression. Modern antidepressants called Selective Serotonin Re-uptake Inhibitors (SSRI) work by increasing the availability of certain chemicals associated with a good mood.

Two broad theories are suggested to account for why a person's brain chemistry may become altered in depression: these are the *Genetic* and the *Evolutionary* theories.

Genetic Theory of Depression

The 'genetic' view proposes that some individuals are constitutionally more inclined to become depressed due to a genetic sensitivity they have inherited. Our genes control those chemical processes that occur in the brain, and it is possible that a malfunction in the way key neurochemicals are produced leads to an individual becoming depressed. Antidepressants are believed to correct this malfunction and their success is often cited as evidence to support this genetic theory.

If it is true that our genetic make-up causes depression then it should be the case that people with a similar genetic make-up should be equally prone to depression. To investigate this, researchers have focused carefully on the experience of identical twins. According to the genetic explanation for depression, it would be naturally expected that where one of the twins becomes depressed the other should also. The evidence from research is that this is broadly the case, with 50 per cent of identical twins likely to become depressed if the other twin is diagnosed with this problem. This is much more than one would expect in the general population and suggests that there may well be genetic factors at work in depression. The conclusion from this research is that while genetics may render some people more susceptible to depression than others, many factors are likely to be involved in converting a genetic sensitivity to an actual episode of clinical depression.

Evolutionary Theory and the 'Depressed Brain'

Professor Paul Gilbert in his book *Overcoming Depression* suggests a unique explanation for how we may become depressed. He looks to evolutionary theory and describes how both biological and psychological factors interact to cause depression. His basic idea is that we are programmed to switch into certain brain states if circumstances require it. Thus we have an innate potential to become anxious in situations where we feel threatened in some way. The body automatically secretes adrenaline to alert us immediately to possible danger and this hormone energises us to take evasive action. There are other types of situations which may trigger a 'depressive response', where the brain switches into a state where we experience low energy, low mood and a tendency to withdraw into ourselves. This 'depressed brain state' is activated in situations where we experience the loss of a loved one, and in certain no-win situations where we feel forced to do things we don't want to do out of fear (enforced subordination) or where we feel trapped over an extended period of time. As Professor Gilbert describes: 'If we are in unhappy marriages or terrible jobs or live in a place that we hate but can't get away from, we can come to feel that we are stuck, with no way out.' Another way that the 'depressed brain' can be activated is when we demand perfection of ourselves and constantly aim too high in our aspirations. Since the expectations we put on ourselves can never be achieved we constantly feel a sense of failure and defeat.

When these depressed states of mind are activated the brain chemistry changes and we become drawn into predictable patterns of gloom. In the same way as we can exaggerate experiences of anxiety by filling our minds with catastrophic images of all the bad things that could possibly happen to us, we can amplify a depressed state of mind by heaping self-criticism and self-blame upon ourselves for how we are feeling, ignoring those circumstances which provoked the crisis. Medications may serve to lift us out of these states of mind, but at some point the circumstances which provoked them also need to be addressed.

The more severe the episode of depression the more likely it is that there are biological factors at work. Thus, episodes of depression are particularly deemed to be 'biological' when they occur in someone who has a diagnosis of Manic Depression, a condition which produces a mood disorder with varying episodes of mania, characterised by a variety of symptoms including inappropriate elation, extreme motor activity, impulsiveness, excessively rapid speech, and severe episodes of depression, as described above. The enormous benefit that specific medications bring to these individuals is evidence that neurochemical imbalances are key factors in this disorder.

Summary

Depression is believed to result from certain vulnerabilities becoming activated in the individual. An individual's early life experience may have left them with negative beliefs about their worth and rigid rules which they feel compelled to live by to ensure some measure of self-esteem and acceptance by others. At some point it becomes impossible to fulfil the terms of these rules of living and their underlying sense of being unloved, unwanted or inadequate overwhelms them and draws them into depression. Genetic factors which they have inherited may also leave them uniquely vulnerable to changes in brain chemistry which regulate our moods. Finally, negative social circumstances with which one is struggling may produce feelings of being trapped and helpless which can easily draw us into a depressed state of mind.

For most individuals it may take a combination of the above factors to produce an episode of depression. Treatment may require that you give attention to each of the factors that have contributed to your particular experience. Recovery takes time and you may need to be modest in your expectations of yourself for the first month or so. Above all you should feel safe with whoever you confide in, and feel that they understand not just what you tell them, but the hurt you feel in your heart which can seem impossible to put into words.

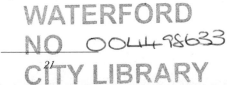

Self-help Exercise

Depression can be experienced in different ways and to different degrees. Once you have identified that it is a problem for you, a first step might be to talk to a trusted friend or counsellor in the coming week. This will help you to break the spell of isolation upon which depression feeds, and access some support and advice. One of the most self-defeating reactions people have when they become depressed is to withdraw into themselves and endure their private hell alone. Depression feeds on the soil of shame and secrecy. Put another way, expression is the great enemy of depression. The more open we are with ourselves and others about how we feel, the greater the chance we can change how we feel.

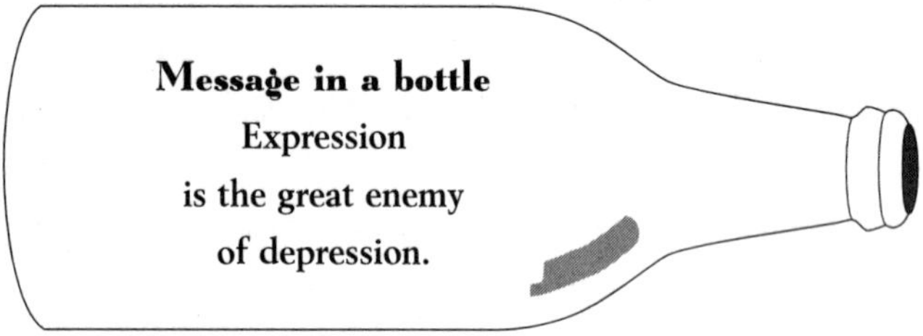
Message in a bottle
Expression
is the great enemy
of depression.

CHAPTER 3

A Major Obstacle to Recovery: Hopelessness

Sarah's Recovery Journal
Excerpt 3

I can't do anything any more. Anytime I attempt to work I clog up inside and leave it. I don't do anything because I don't think that I can. There's no point, it's all so hopeless. Even if I do try I get nowhere. I have absolutely no belief in myself any more. There's no hope in my heart, there's no happiness in my thoughts. I feel as if I'm tied up and can't break loose. I'm too afraid to do anything because I think I'll fail and it'll only make me feel worse, and so I do nothing. But that makes me feel so bad because all I do is sit around and do nothing. I'm so lazy. I don't understand anything. What's the point? It's all so useless, and worthless and utterly hopeless and I hate it. I'm so afraid.

What hurts most when you are depressed is the compelling feeling you experience that there will never be an end to your suffering. You can never imagine experiencing again the peace of mind and inner joy which other people talk about. This belief that there can be no change, no easing of the burden, no light to shatter the darkness, creates a feeling of hopelessness.

Hopelessness generates a mindset which defeats you even before you start. It saps your energy and convinces you that nothing is worth trying, that nothing will make any difference. Even if you do try, you believe you will fail. Your will to struggle is overcome by negative thoughts that induce despair: 'What's the point, I'm such a loser' or 'It doesn't matter what I do, no one cares anyway.' The fact that you regard these thoughts as completely true is understandable but dangerous. Hopelessness fractures your sense of trust both in yourself and in life and it locks you into a personal despair. We can picture hopelessness as a vicious cycle where negative feelings and inactivity feed on one another to convince you nothing is worth trying:

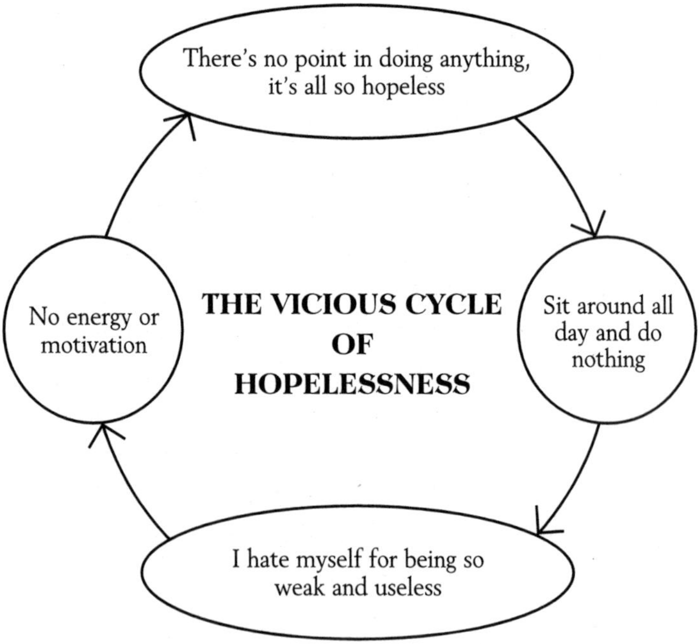
There's no point in doing anything, it's all so hopeless
Sit around all day and do nothing
I hate myself for being so weak and useless
No energy or motivation
THE VICIOUS CYCLE OF HOPELESSNESS

In this chapter we will consider other ways of looking at your situation which may loosen the grip of hopelessness and overcome the sense of defeat it generates.

Think in Terms of 'Possibilities'

Ciaran was a 29-year-old man with a long history of depression. He had been attending the outpatient clinic faithfully for over eight years when, one day, he broke down during his session with the psychiatrist and asked if there was something more that he could do besides taking the prescribed medication. He was referred for psychotherapy and after some weeks he spoke of his profound conviction that he was 'a stupid, fat, ugly bastard'. Nothing seemed to shift this core conviction. One day I asked him how he would like to think of himself as a person if he could wake up tomorrow with his problems all resolved. He was surprised but also saddened by this question. He seemed to find it impossible to actually say anything positive about himself so I suggested he write down his answer. He took a writing pad and wrote down three words: 'intelligent', 'funny (sort of)' and 'caring'. With his permission I read these words back to him and his face took on an expression of intense anguish. He was upset and he could hardly speak. He eventually explained that deep down part of him wanted to believe that these positive attributes were true of himself, but that he became unbearably sad if he tried to do so.

Somehow it was less painful to write himself off as a hopeless case than to believe that there might be some goodness in him. His hopelessness was protective in some ways but it was also like a dense bed of weeds that blocked any possibility of colour and beauty blossoming within him. Together we tried to find a way of thinking that could create some space for him to recover. After many unsuccessful efforts we hit on a simple strategy that made a huge difference. Rather than argue with his negative beliefs, which he resisted strongly, we agreed that he would consider two possibilities: one was that he was indeed a 'complete loser' and the other that he was 'a human being who thought he was a complete loser'. The second option did not deny his negative thoughts but it highlighted the possibility that this was one way of thinking about himself and that there might be other ways. For the first time Ciaran relaxed and smiled. He said he could 'buy this' and his mind became open to considering how he could think more hopefully about his present and his future. Certainly he could accept that he was a human being who was hurting and deeply conflicted about his own basic goodness. His sense of despair lifted slightly and we were able to proceed and explore alternative ways in which he could view himself other than constantly writing himself off as loathsome.

Approach Old Problems in New Ways

A common problem that depressed people report initially in therapy is the feeling that their lives are overwhelming. There is too much to do and they cannot see any way of meeting certain demands and completing tasks that others expect of them. One of the reasons that life can seem overwhelming to any one of us is that we think in global terms of all the things that have to be done, rather than in specific terms about the different tasks that require our attention. Writing down the different stresses you face and standing back from them can reduce the sense of being overwhelmed. This sounds simple but for someone with depression it can be hard to stand back and look at anything objectively since you feel so trapped. But if you can begin to make a list of the different stresses that you are facing, you will see clearly that there is a limited rather than an infinite number of things you have to do, and this realisation may reduce your stress level significantly. You can decide what can be ignored for the present and what needs your immediate attention and you can start thinking in terms of a realistic timeframe within which you might expect to deal with this. Depression often leads people to have very unrealistic expectations of themselves, so be careful to give yourself slightly more time than you may need rather than slightly less. Remember too that it is not necessary to think that 'It's all up to me.' It may well be that there are people or other kinds of support that would make the completion of a particular task much more feasible and enjoyable.

Take a sheet of paper and write your list of 'Things needing my attention'. When you have completed this exercise, consider where you will find time to complete any particular task and what is going to help you most settle down to this task. If, for example, you need to write a letter, it might be important to consider making a space for yourself to do this, where interruptions are minimised and where you have time to think about what you need to say. It might also be important to plan to spend a short amount of time at this task rather than trying to force yourself to complete it all at one go. Depression reduces our ability to concentrate and you will very likely find your mind wanders after a relatively short period.

By setting up your expectations of yourself in very modest and reasonable ways it is far more likely you will be successful in achieving your goal. If you think you should take exercise and you consider that you should walk at least three miles a day to make this worth while, plan to walk one mile a day, three days a week and see how that feels. Note how easy it is to be contemptuous of such a small step. Try not to give in to this self-contempt. The most important thing is that you can set some goal, no matter how small, and accomplish it. Nothing succeeds like success. It restores morale, breaks the cycle of procrastination, and enables you to see possibilities for coming to terms with other stresses in your life that have overwhelmed you. Recovery involves breaking the grip of hopelessness by setting up some realistic expectations and finding that you can meet these expectations of yourself. Success is the achievement of small things, accomplishing everyday mundane tasks that seem impossible. That's success.

Focus on Positive Past Memories and Specific Future Events You Can Look Forward To

An interesting finding from research on hopelessness and depression is reported in a book by Professor Mark Williams, *Cry of Pain*. His research showed that individuals who feel hopeless do not actually spend their time thinking of negative things that may happen in their futures. What sets them apart from other, non-depressed people is the absence of any positive events that they can see in their futures. The 'painful future' they contemplate is not the anticipation of negative events, but rather a future without any positive events. This finding would suggest that to help combat hopelessness it is not enough to try to stop thinking negatively, but rather there is a need to try to envision specific concrete positive events that might make your future more bearable. Give yourself permission to dream and do not be afraid to do so.

Ask yourself what it would take to make your immediate future bearable. Be as specific and concrete as you can. And then, looking a little further down the road, what would you like to see happen over the next few months or year that would give you a sense that this depression is worth struggling through. Again, be very specific. Looking to the future and hoping for something like 'that I would feel happier in myself' is not specific enough, even though it is a perfectly reasonable wish. Something like 'being at dinner with someone with whom I feel comfortable and at ease' is much more likely to provide a realistic focus for you and something which you could genuinely believe to be a possibility that can be achieved.

Refuse to Accept that You Somehow Deserve to Feel Depressed

It is very common for people who are depressed and hopeless to feel that they somehow 'deserve' what's happening to them.

They can be convinced that they have done something wrong in the past which has resulted in them feeling the way they do and therefore they should simply 'put up with it'. The feeling that you somehow deserve to be in pain clearly robs you of any energy to fight back and to believe that you have the right to be happy.

No one *deserves* to feel depressed. We can all experience sadness and hurt feelings from time to time. But depression is not about feeling a little sad. It is a complex of very negative emotions that cloud the mind and distort our vision of who we are. It condemns us to a very lonely place within ourselves where no one can reach us and where we can't even seem to reach ourselves.

It is not your fault that you are depressed. It is possible to understand and resolve the pain you are in. Some set of circumstances has stirred your deepest insecurities leaving you with doubts about your worth, competence and goodness as a human being. People who are depressed are very often described as being terribly selfish. While it is true that their thoughts seem to centre exclusively on themselves, and that their behaviour might seem very self-centred, it is not accurate to say they are 'selfish'. Depression generates such pain within the soul that the sufferer is unable to focus their mind outside themselves and invest in activities and people around them.

Be Open to Being Surprised

Hopelessness may also stem from a difficulty in believing that life is fair. The losses you have experienced, the setbacks and failures that you have endured, may well lead you to feel that you are alone in a very uncaring world. Anger and hurt can turn to obstinacy and a refusal to engage in any kind of self-help activities. You feel that your pain is so unfair and that you shouldn't have to struggle with it. Or you may feel that too much seems to depend on you and that there seems to be so little support available. Trying to recover may seem simply another burden which you do not need.

What's missing in these thoughts is any sense that life may surprise you in your recovery and meet you part-way in your struggle. It may be something very simple — something you read, a chance meeting with an old friend, a conversation where you feel genuinely accepted and affirmed, or an employment opportunity which opens up new possibilities for you. Recovery depends as much on these everyday 'graces' as it does upon your effort. But what life may provide by way of a 'grace' can so easily be missed if your mindset becomes embittered and closed. The primary responsibility to struggle with depression is yours but it's not all up to you. Life will give you some breaks — watch out for them.

Summary

Hopelessness is the belief that nothing in yourself or in life can change the way you feel. It saps your energy and makes you feel defeated before you even start. It's a major obstacle in fighting depression and the following key points may help:

- Break problems down into small steps.
- Deal with one thing at a time.
- Focus on what you can do rather than what you can't do.
- Recall specific past events which made you happy and consider what could happen in the future that would mean something to you.
- Trust that life can give you a break when you least expect it to.

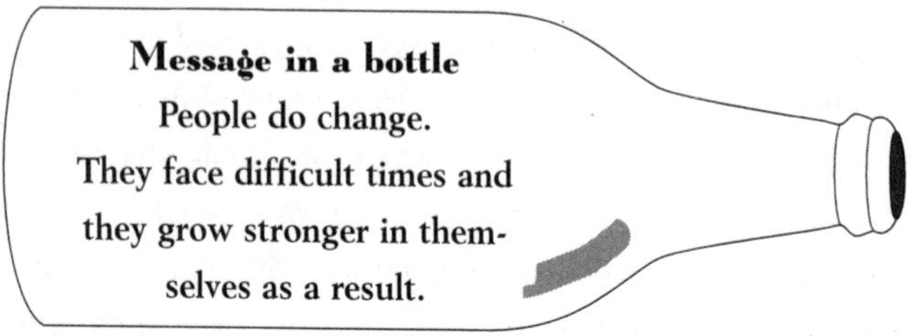
Message in a bottle
People do change.
They face difficult times and
they grow stronger in them-
selves as a result.

CHAPTER 4

Overcoming Depression: A Recovery Plan

If you have been depressed for any length of time you have probably tried different methods to 'shake it off'. You may have found some things work, if only for a while. Distraction can be a welcome visitor and break the grip of morbid self-preoccupation. Sleep can be a great healer, particularly when it restores energy to tackle what has been avoided. Music can be a comfort — sitting with a lighted candle and listening to some piece which both resonates with and lifts your mood. A friend who is easy to be with, a pet who adores you unconditionally, a God who believes in you and invites you to believe in yourself, a walk by the sea that calms your mind and lets you find some realistic perspective on problems. However, these strategies may fail to sustain a positive mood over time and it becomes apparent that a clear focused recovery plan is required.

What follows is an overview of such a recovery plan that attempts to integrate physical, psychological, emotional and interpersonal strategies for overcoming clinical depression. Because the experience of depression is so individual, some strategies may be more relevant for you than others. Thus, for some people medication is essential in helping them lift themselves out of the gloom they are experiencing. For others, dealing with patterns of negative thinking and learning to relate to others in healthier ways may be what brings relief. If you have been lacking energy and unable to deal with important tasks the next chapter, 'Getting Started', may be particularly relevant. Below is a short overview of each of these different strategies.

Physical Treatments for Depression

Many of the symptoms of depression are physical in nature, and there is evidence that some people are constitutionally more vulnerable to this disorder where there is a clear family history of depression in close relatives. Because of this, many professional health carers believe that treatment of depression should begin with attempting to change the physical chemistry of the body. Depletion in the availability of certain neurotransmitters has been linked to depression and medications are available which specifically target levels of these neurotransmitters in the brain. Newer medications such as Prozac and Seroxat increase the availability of serotonin and this is believed to directly affect the negative mood that one experiences when depressed. There are other antidepressant medications which target slightly different neurotransmitters and each has its own particular benefits according to the symptom profile of an individual at a given time.

Sufferers may become uneasy when the option of medical treatment is presented. They may feel that their problems have been around for a long time and that there may well be elements in their childhood history or their current lifestyle which are directly contributing to their low mood. Concern is often expressed about the possibility of becoming dependent on medication and therefore requiring long-term maintenance treatment over the course of their life.

The key benefit of medication is that for many people it can help relieve the physical symptoms that characterise depression in a relatively short time. Medication cannot correct social or personality factors that have contributed to the sufferer becoming depressed, and counselling can be important to explore these factors.

How the option of medication is presented to the individual is important. One metaphor which I often discuss with patients is that of a lifebelt. When someone is drowning they need something to lift them safely above water and get them out of danger. This intervention will not necessarily teach them how to swim, nor will it help them understand why they fell into deep water. There is important work to be done along with medication to investigate all the reasons for the crisis and to help sufferers prevent future relapses.

It is unfortunate that the dogmatism that characterises many professionals working in this field of treatment does not always make available a holistic recovery programme for depression. Medical and non-medical practitioners can actively dissuade the individual from pursing either a course of medication or psychotherapy, which naturally confuses the sufferer. Heated argument has been evident for years in the medical community with some believing that depression is an exclusive biological illness that requires exclusive treatment by medication. On the other hand there are those who feel it to be an expression of key issues in a person's life that require exploration and resolution. Many psychotherapists and counsellors are wary of medication because they worry it diverts attention away from these issues.

The picture is somewhat clearer when one looks to the research on what constitutes effective treatment for depression. Results of numerous studies would conclude that some forms of psychotherapy are as effective as medication in reducing symptoms of depression, but that the combination of medication and therapy seems to be more beneficial than either one alone. Psychotherapy has also been found to decrease vulnerability to relapse while relapse is very likely when medication is discontinued and personality problems are left unresolved. Medication may be particularly important to consider where the sufferer reports an intense experience of pain, a family history of depression, or strong suicidal feelings.

If you are looking for someone professional to treat your depression try to find someone who seems enlightened, respectful of other therapeutic approaches, and willing to consider what your particular experience of depression may require in order for you to achieve a full recovery. A good GP is the starting place for most sufferers and generally he or she can advise on medication and arrange a referral to appropriate specialists on your behalf.

Besides the potential benefit of antidepressant medication, there are other physical means of helping to alter your mood and support your recovery. Physical exercise has been found to alter brain chemistry and can enhance mood; nutrition can be an important element in recovery, particularly since someone in the grip of depression can completely overlook the importance of a balanced diet. Finding ways of truly relaxing one's body and one's mind through meditation, aromatherapy, reflexology and sleep may be key in restoring some level of energy and motivation to face life.

Seeking Help from a Therapist

A counsellor or psychotherapist may be crucial in helping you make a lasting recovery from depression. Counselling offers a space where you can be listened to with respect and explore ways to help you find your way through the darkness. Psychotherapy offers a structured programme for overcoming depression but it also seeks to uncover some of the root causes of depression which make you vulnerable to repeated experiences with this disorder.

Recovery involves becoming open to what is troubling you at an emotional level. Painful feelings and associated painful memories often require a safe setting within which you can confide in another and gain the support you need to talk through what has been avoided for so long. Unwanted feelings and memories are often avoided because people feel they will be too much to bear. The support of a counsellor or friend can enable you to gradually tease out what is most troubling in your history and in your inner life and give you the strength to face these fears. Finding someone who can listen intelligently and sensitively to one's inner struggle can often be difficult. Very often friends will be supportive and sympathetic but they can only go so far in helping you tease out underlying feelings that are not so obvious. The availability of a therapist who can give you undivided attention for fifty minutes can be enormously important in helping you listen to yourself and make connections with what has been troubling you over many years and what is troubling you now.

Besides seeking support and considering specialist help which may involve medication or some form of physical care, recovery from depression may require you to employ a number of different strategies. The diagram below illustrates a holistic plan which highlights each of these different elements of recovery:

STRATEGIES FOR OVERCOMING DEPRESSION

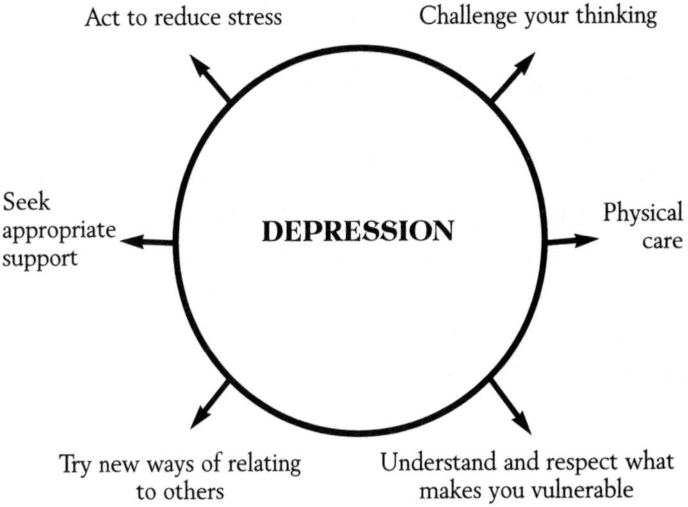

Reduce Stress

Depressed patients are usually confronted with multiple pressures which need to be eased to make recovery possible. In reviewing your current life situation consider in what practical ways you might reduce stress. Often very simple actions can make a big difference. Postponing certain duties that do not require immediate attention, cancelling unimportant events, arranging to take a weekend off, finding out exactly where you stand in relation to some matter so that you can stop worrying about it, or asking help of friends, can help greatly ease your situation.

Challenge Your Negative Thinking

Negative thinking patterns, such as constant self-criticism, can contribute directly towards maintaining a depressed mood and they can become habitual for a person over time. By 'catching' these negative thoughts, and considering other ways of thinking that are more compassionate, optimistic and realistic towards yourself, you begin to see your life in a more hopeful way. Sometimes, by simply noting these repetitive thoughts and saying to yourself, 'There I go again!' you can stop them taking control of your mood and dragging you down.

Know Where Your Vulnerabilities Lie

Underlying the experience of depression are beliefs about ourselves and other people which are often the root cause of the problem. Understanding the origin of these beliefs and knowing where you are most vulnerable can make it easier to accept and take care of yourself. Depression can result when your deepest insecurities about yourself become active and dominate your thinking.

Try New Ways of Relating to Others

Negative patterns of relating to others where you feel overly responsible for others, overly concerned with meeting their expectations and gaining their approval, can also leave you constantly vulnerable to feeling a sense of failure, which can contribute to depression.

The Pattern of Recovery from Depression

People emerge from depression feeling tremendous relief and feeling stronger in themselves. It is important to keep this in mind but also to be gentle with yourself and to be patient with the time recovery may require. For some it can be quite rapid, particularly when an obvious stress in their life is resolved or when medication seems to 'hit the spot' and lift one's mood. But for the majority of sufferers recovery can be a matter of two steps forward, one step back. Their mood lifts significantly for a period of time but good days are followed for a time by gloomy days. Energy which seems to be available to them for an evening can be curiously absent the next morning. Self-esteem which recovers following some successful experience may falter a day later when they are unable to manage some new aspect of their life.

I remember one man who became quite frustrated with me during recovery because his moods were very unpredictable for a period of time. During one session he said, 'In any given week I have about four good days and three bad ones. The problem is I never can predict how I'll be tomorrow. Before I started therapy I felt miserable seven days a week, but at least life was predictable!'

Below are two diagrams which illustrate (a) what people can often imagine recovery to look like and (b) what recovery actually is like:

(a) Recovery is rarely like this: ***(b) Recovery is more like this:***

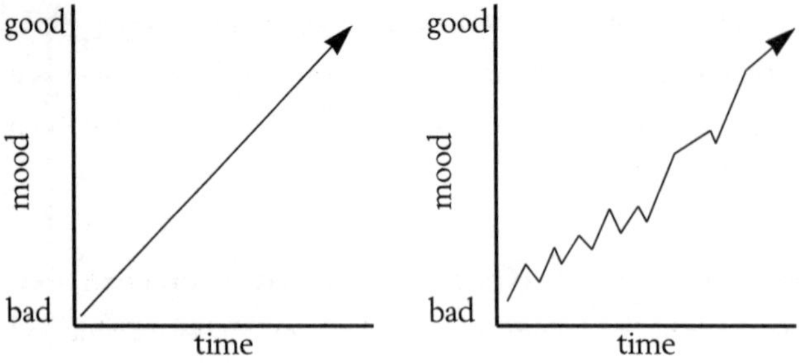

Keeping a Recovery Journal

One strategy which can be very helpful in the course of your recovery is to keep a diary or journal. I often recommend buying a large notebook and making entries on a daily basis. For those of you who have ready access to a computer, it may be convenient to open a file — a 'recovery file'. What you write about may vary quite considerably depending on whatever is important to you on a given day. For example, you may want to write about how badly you are feeling, or you may want to write out some practical ways you found to improve your mood. Remember to give yourself credit for even the smallest successes and achievements you've had in struggling with this problem. Each step you take in recovery, no matter how small, is significant and worth noting. On the days you feel like writing longer entries, you may reflect on some of the experiences in your life that might have left you vulnerable to depression.

You have already been introduced to 'Sarah', who had been suffering with depression for over a year when we picked up her story. She was attending university when she came for help and she complained of feeling down, being unable to concentrate and withdrawing from friends. Soon after she started therapy it became clear that her problems were complex and her mood much more depressed than it had initially appeared.

Sarah's Recovery Journal

Excerpt 4

I want to live. I want to care and I want to love. I want to be capable of failing but not falling apart. And I want warmth. I want to feel loved and cared for not neglected and ignored. I want to know and learn how not to neglect and ignore myself. I'd like to be me. By writing this journal and asking to have someone read it I realise I'm asking to be listened to, to be heard, to be read, to be understood, to be treated as a living person who is hurting so much inside and needs to be cared for and who needs some kind of compassion to help me keep going and discover some way to ground myself. This notebook says more than any verbal discourse because it's a concentrated effort of really writing down how I am. It's true it's painful and it hurts to do this but at least I'm now allowing this pain to surface. For most of my life I've refused to acknowledge my feelings and this has distorted my sense of myself. I've not been able to have any clear sense of who I am but since I've allowed myself to write things down I've become much clearer about the person that I am inside.

Writing is becoming a comfort to me. It's a space on paper where I can express myself without any judgment at all. It is a sanctuary of hope where I can begin to discover things I do not know about myself. It's a labyrinth of words, thousands upon thousands, which I have needed to relocate a sense of myself. I need to write so much. I have to. It's only when I write that I begin to effectively identify something about the way I feel and in so doing I become more definite about who I am.

A consultation with a psychiatrist was arranged and she began a course of medication. One month later she still complained of suicidal feelings and it was agreed with her that hospital admission would be helpful to allow her a safe place in which to recover. Writing about her experience of recovery proved to be very helpful to Sarah. The amount she wrote varied greatly from day to day. Some days she felt incredibly despondent, and on others there was evidence of hope and strength returning. Excerpt 4 from her journal above conveys how keeping a journal helped her to discover a stronger sense of herself.

Message in a bottle
Recovery is about finding a door in
the wall that surrounds you.

CHAPTER 5

Getting Started

Doing one thing, one thing at a time

Depression can be a paralysing experience. You notice your mood turning dark and you realise that you're slipping into that place where everything feels too much, where you lack the energy to think clearly and to sort out whatever problems beset you. Your mood colours your thinking, your thoughts become more negative, and your body feels physically sore as you get drawn into a lonely isolated place inside yourself. You know you're not making any headway in 'getting a grip' and you think: 'Here we go again, my life is a complete mess and there is nothing I can do about it.' You want to stay put, do nothing, because you are convinced that to try to do anything would only make it worse. In fact, nothing could be further from the truth.

Research has shown when we become depressed we are most likely to react to our negative moods in the following way: we focus our attention on how we are *feeling*, rather than on what we could *do* to ease our stress. Our behaviour is driven completely by our negative mood — 'If I don't *feel* I can handle it, it probably means I shouldn't even try.' We procrastinate and convince ourselves that 'I'll do it later when I *feel* more like doing it.'

The problem with this way of thinking is that it assumes that the feeling or *motivation* for doing something should come before you actually do anything. While this may be true when you're feeling positive about life, it's exactly the opposite when you are depressed. In a low mood, the motivation to do anything comes only once you've started into the task. Action precedes motivation. If you set about doing something that you've been avoiding and take even very small steps towards achieving your goal, you may be surprised at how the energy for that task does come in the doing of it.

Bad moods are the result of becoming aware of what indeed may be a real issue in our lives at a moment when we're least able to think clearly and honestly about it. We are simply too tired, too alone, too agitated or too gloomy. We think about the problem in the worst light possible and work ourselves into complete despair as we fail to see how it can be resolved. When you get into this kind of a rut you need to do something to distract yourself for a little while until your body has recovered. When you feel very tired you may be particularly vulnerable. At such moments no amount of logical argument can enable you to get the right perspective on your life situation. The head cannot reassure the heart.

On these occasions what can help most is doing something very practical and physical. Tidying up, preparing a meal, fixing a fire, writing a simple letter to a friend, paying a bill. Sleep can also work wonders to restore a true perspective on things. But many sufferers find that sleep does not come easily. In his recovery journal, John described how he had managed to stop himself slipping into misery by taking some practical steps to distract himself from worrying about an upsetting problem:

> Today was a bad day for me as I couldn't stop worrying about a problem which I was not in a position to resolve. It wasn't really my problem, but it concerned someone I cared about. I couldn't let go my concerns, and I noticed myself slipping into a most depressing outlook on the whole situation.

I decided that some distraction was in order. I started by ringing a friend and chatting about something entirely different for ten minutes. I then took myself off for a short walk. My mood was still 'down' but along the way I got chatting to some neighbours, who were repairing their hall door. They kindly invited me in for tea. Perhaps it was the break, perhaps it was the tea, but I actually feel that it was the human contact which restored some sanity and allowed me let go of what had previously seemed so oppressive. I still cared about the situation that remained unresolved, but it no longer consumed me, and I could see hopeful possibilities where before I could only see tragedy.

There are some specific things you can do to help you get through a bad day. We'll take them one by one:

(a) *Step one:* Putting some structure into your day.
(b) *Step two:* Ensuring there is some human contact in your day.
(c) *Step three:* Building in some time to reflect on how things worked out for you.

These suggestions are aimed at helping you make it through the day and restoring some sense of you being in control of your life. Taking responsibility for one day at a time is as much as you can manage at this stage. And each day you do this will bring you one step closer to recovery. As your mood gradually improves you can explore more about what has led to you becoming depressed. There are probably one or two critical issues in your life that have made you vulnerable to depression. When your inner strength returns it will be easier to identify and confront these deeper issues.

Step One: Putting Some Structure on Your Day

One of the most consistent findings in the studies on different treatments for depression is that **activity helps our moods**. Why not experiment and see if this finding holds true for you?

Because we rarely feel like being active when we are depressed, activities have to be planned ahead of time. Almost every self-help book on depression you pick up has some form of daily diary you can fill in to help you plan a schedule of activities from morning to night. The simple single day planner I've included on p. 51 has an outline of the day taking one hour at a time.

Don't aim too high, and be fairly sure that you can complete the tasks which you set yourself today. Write in a couple of potentially constructive activities that will be likely to give you some sense of accomplishment (aim for two each day) and then fill in the hours around them as you go through the day with whatever you happen to do. A word or two is all that's necessary to describe any activity, e.g. 'breakfast', 'walk', 'clean desk', 'visit friend', 'watch favourite TV programme'.

Nothing succeeds like success for someone who is depressed. If you do set yourself some goals today and complete them, particularly one or two activities that will give you a sense of accomplishment, you'll find yourself in a far better frame of mind afterwards to face tomorrow.

There is one other aspect to this exercise which should make it more interesting for you. When you fill in your diary as you go through the day, rate on a scale of 0 to 100 how depressed you felt during that hour. Imagine this scale in your mind and choose a rating for each hour which feels right to you.

To summarise, this exercise is called 'Activity Scheduling', and it involves three features:

Daily Activity Schedule

- At the beginning of each day, or the night before, write in your diary one or two activities that are likely to give you some feeling of satisfaction or accomplishment.
- Complete your diary as you go through the day by noting down a word or two to describe how you spend each hour.
- Rate how your mood felt during each hour on the following 0 to 100 scale:

0	10	20	30	40	50	60	70	80	90	100
Not at all depressed										The most depressed I've ever been

What You May Learn from Activity Scheduling

You may find over a few days of completing this exercise that you begin to notice certain connections between how you spend your time and your mood. The first thing to check is whether your mood varies or whether it just stays exactly the same regardless of what you do. If it varies, what does this say about your depression? You may notice that your mood reacts positively to certain conditions. Perhaps you can ease your pain by moving towards certain kinds of activities and letting go other activities.

If the research is right you should discover that the more active you are, the less depressed you feel. Is this what you found? Why do you think this might be the case? Did you find that there were times when you moved from feeling very down during one hour of the day, to feeling much brighter an hour later? What kinds of activities were associated with these positive mood shifts? You might want to make a note in your 'recovery journal' about what you're learning from this exercise.

Here are some things that one man learned from monitoring his moods and relating them to how he spent his time. Having kept an activity diary for a full week he noticed the following patterns:

- My really bad times were in the evenings when I sat in the living room chair and appeared to my family to doze off. In fact I was not sleeping, but withdrawing from everyone.
- Once I let my mood sink into a dark place, I found it stayed that way for hours.
- The times I felt best were times when I walked my two racing dogs, and also those times when I felt I had made some important contribution at work.
- Exercise in particular seemed to lift my spirits, but I never really wanted to exercise and when I did it took nearly an hour of walking before the benefits were noticeable.
- Perhaps the most important thing I learned was that action does precede motivation. It was only after starting to do something that I felt any energy and interest in doing it. When you're depressed it's not at all a good idea to wait around until you *feel* like doing something. Just do it, the motivation will kick in soon after you start.

Often what helps is planning some novel activity which breaks your normal routine. Consider including in your week some activity you've been meaning to try but have never quite got around to. You might plan to attend a music concert or you might attend some neighbourhood meeting and learn what's planned for your area. The point is to consider breaking your usual routine and trying out some new behaviour.

WHAT CAN I DO WHEN I FEEL REALLY DOWN?

Distract myself

Make a 'to do' list

Do one thing

Do it badly
(rather than not at all)

Talk to someone

Plan something pleasurable in my day

Step Two: Include Some Human Nurturing in Your Daily Plan

One individual whom I treated in an outpatient group for depression shared with others that he believed 'We all live our lives too much alone in our heads.' This is probably true for most of us, but it can be an especially lonely experience for the depressed person. An important element of recovery which is emphasised throughout this book concerns the need to move out of isolation towards genuine, life-giving contact with others. Solitude can restore the human spirit, but when you're depressed, solitude can magnify your negative thinking and before you know it, you have slipped into a frightening despair.

At some point each day consider how you might spend some time in the company of friends. Some brief time of being with others in a light-hearted, friendly way could help to lift your spirits. Perhaps you could visit someone who themselves needs some company; perhaps a phone call to an old friend you haven't been in touch with for some time. Or you might pop into a neighbour's house and soak up the atmosphere of warmth and fun that fills their home.

Step Three: Building in Some Time for Personal Reflection

Depression has a dreadful memory for the good things that happen to us, and a wonderful memory for things that went wrong, or that afterwards *you* decided had gone wrong. We call this 'selective attention'. The negative mind filters out all that's not been right and recalls only what it perceives as proof that the 'bottom line' is true. Every depressed person has their own particular 'bottom line'. For some it's the belief that they're not 'lovable', for others it's the belief that 'Nobody really cares about me,' for others it may be that 'There's nothing I can do for myself that will make a difference to how I feel.'

To correct this selective attention, it can be helpful to make notes in your recovery journal about what worked for you today. Was there anything that happened that disproved your 'bottom line'? Can you recall an event which lifted your spirits, or some experience that showed you that you're capable of managing certain aspects of your life effectively? Record these experiences and consider what they reveal about what's life-giving for you, no matter how simple they may be.

You can also learn something useful from experiences that were negative. Perhaps you bit off more than you could chew at this time. What may need to be changed are your expectations of yourself. Could you be expecting even more of yourself when you're depressed than you would if you were feeling good? Are you pushing yourself unreasonably because you feel you have to make up for being so miserable inside? Remember all you are struggling with, and credit yourself for making the effort and succeeding to whatever degree you can.

The suggestion that you take some time to process what happened during the day is another important component of recovery. Accept that you are living through a painful experience and that by taking time to read, reflect and write about your experience, you will gradually find a way out of this prison.

Sarah's Recovery Journal
Excerpt 5

I spent the day in the flat as my cough was quite bad and I didn't feel like going into college to exhaust myself. I had breakfast, watched some TV, ironed and tidied my clothes and then did a translation for homework which took hours. I was happy to have completed this although I still have to check it for grammar mistakes. Although it took me so long to do this work and I know I have a huge amount of work to catch up with, I don't seem to feel that bad about it. Tonight I feel quite relaxed. I think part of this is because I was alone for most of the day and I got something done which made me feel productive.

I wonder where my feelings are hiding tonight because it's unlike me to write so much factual stuff. I'd love it if one day I were to sit down and put pen to paper producing pages and pages about my feelings. I'd love to unblock parts of me that are so afraid of opening. I wouldn't want to open each little door inside of me but I want to see the names on those doors and at least see inside some of those rooms. I'd like to know what's there. I'd like to see what's hiding inside. I don't want to always be afraid of holding these feelings back. I want to let them live inside me.

For some people, writing may not come so easily. This is certainly the case when depression is felt intensely. You can't concentrate enough to write, your mind wanders, and you find yourself getting caught up in negative ruminations over which you have little control. During these times the emphasis in your recovery has to be on *doing* things that bring relief. Take a walk, listen to or play some music, find a quiet bench in a local park, or if you can, get down to the sea, watch the incoming tide, and let your mind become calmed by the beauty of it all. Later, when your mood has slightly lifted, see if you can write a little about what has been happening for you, and what seems to be helping.

The excerpt from Sarah's journal above reflects the benefit she gained from attending to some everyday chores and to some homework she'd been putting off. Her comments at the end of this entry reveal questions she was beginning to ask herself concerning her deeper feelings. She would explore these issues more at a later stage of her recovery, but her mention of them in this entry suggested she was feeling strong enough in herself to at least ask these questions and not feel so frightened of her inner life.

Self-help Suggestions

- Don't leave it to depression to plan your day. Take control, put some structure on the day and be sure to plan to do two activities that are likely to give you a sense of personal accomplishment.
- Spend some time in the company of friends and draw on their warmth.
- Reflect on what you learned from the day. If you can't write much, take some 'time out' in whatever way is most relaxing for you and consider what was most life-giving for you today.
- Remember it is very hard to get started on any activity when you feel depressed. Be gentle with yourself and give yourself lots of encouragement when you manage to achieve even 'tiny' steps.

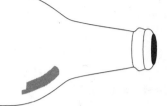

Message in a bottle
Action precedes motivation.

ACTIVITY DIARY

Time	Activity	Rate your mood (0–100*)
9–10 a.m.		
10–11 a.m.		
11–12 a.m.		
12–1 p.m.		
1–2 p.m.		
2–3 p.m.		
3–4 p.m.		
4–5 p.m.		
5–6 p.m.		
6–7 p.m.		
7–8 p.m.		
8–9 p.m.		
9–10 p.m.		
11–12 p.m.		

*0 = Not at all depressed; 100 = Most depressed I've ever been

CHAPTER 6

It's the Thought that Counts

Dealing with negative thinking that keeps you depressed

Peter was in his twenties with a very promising career. Two years beforehand he had stopped work because of vague symptoms of ill health which were eventually diagnosed as being due to depression. He'd been unpopular and bullied at school. His reaction to this had been to adopt an attitude of competitiveness to overcome his fear of rejection by his peers. Winning was how he felt he could gain acceptance. And it worked a lot of the time. However, he drove himself relentlessly in every aspect of his life and he took failure very badly. Anything less than perfection made him annoyed with himself to the point where he would be verbally aggressive with himself. His constant pushing and berating of himself had clearly contributed to his mental exhaustion. 'My being sick', he said, 'allowed me to avoid killing myself by trying so hard at work. My illness is a sign I need to change my life, to stop listening to my mind and try listening to my heart.'

◆◆◆

> At seventeen, with the Leaving Certificate successfully behind her, and a warm attractive personality which drew others to her, Jennifer was highly insecure and prone to severe mood slumps. Her immediate family was marked with a history of chronic depression which had taken its toll on all the children in different ways. But Jennifer was determined to hold on to some semblance of mental health and not succumb to the self-defeating behaviours she observed at home. Frequent battles were waged within her mind between the part of her that wanted to break free from home and the part of her that felt guilty that she wasn't doing more to make those around her 'better'. In those periods where she felt down, she would turn against herself with an attitude of self-loathing, picking on details of her appearance — 'I don't look like any kind of life form until I wear make-up,' her intelligence — 'I am so thick,' and her confusion about her future — 'I don't know what to do with my life.' These thoughts would take hold of her mind, driving her mood into intense hopelessness and provoking her to withdraw from friends who could keep her grounded. What looked initially like normal teenage 'angst' soon became a serious mood problem which lasted for weeks.

Reading the above clips from the lives of two people who were no strangers to depression, you might be tempted to ask many questions regarding what caused their problems. However, I wonder as you read the above accounts can you spot something they both have in common? Something which may not have been the original cause of their depression, but which intensifies their dark moods.

There is a pattern of negative thinking which seemed to drive the emotional upheaval experienced by both Peter and

Jennifer. Depression research and treatment has focused particularly on this feature of the problem and the evidence is that our negative thoughts critically affect our moods, and our behaviour also. With mood problems such as depression, the mind behaves in a fairly predictable and an unhelpful way. Our thinking becomes distorted so that we can no longer see clearly, 'but through a glass darkly'. We turn on ourselves, heaping self-criticism and self-loathing on the 'pathetic' individual we now believe we are; we see the world around us as unsympathetic and unsupportive; and we view our future as a never-ending continuation of our present painful state of mind. Our negative thinking can increase feelings of hopelessness, fear and anger. Our behaviour, in turn, reflects our state of mind and we act in self-defeating ways that lock us into our prison and isolate us from others.

Recovery from depression requires that you become aware of recurrent patterns of negative thinking, and find some way of calming your mind when it becomes so tormented. When your mind is calm, your heart is clear; it's easier to trust yourself and your world. When you trust yourself you begin to see new ways of thinking about your life.

The Link between Thoughts and Moods

In the past twenty years cognitive therapy has been found to work particularly effectively for depression. The word 'cognitive' simply refers to the way we think, the way we look at things. This approach takes as its guiding principle that it is not so much what happens in our life that determines our moods, but rather what an event 'means' to me, that is, how I interpret or view a particular event. My emotional reactions, and how I behave in response to that event, will depend on the unique meaning I give to different situations and moments in my life.

Aaron Beck, the founder of this therapeutic approach, had been working at the University of Pennsylvania in Philadelphia in the 1950s when he began to observe certain features among his depressed patients. He noticed that the thoughts that spontaneously came into their minds in response to any given situation had an immediate impact on how they felt. The thoughts and images — which Beck refers to as 'cognitions' — reported by depressed patients were characteristically self-blaming and defeatist. The thoughts that accompanied anxiety reactions were marked by perceptions of danger and threat to the self. Angry reactions were accompanied by thoughts that perceived others as unfair, or infringing on one's boundary.

Negative patterns of thinking may account for your behaviour in situations which you find difficult. How you 'read' any given situation will determine how you react. If you typically blame yourself for whatever seems wrong, and regard it as 'typical of me', then you will hardly be motivated to deal with that situation constructively. You may push yourself to 'put up' with the situation and 'to stop complaining' about what can't be changed. As a result you feel even more trapped and helpless than before and your mood sinks deeper into depression. Discovering new ways of thinking opens up new possibilities for responding creatively to difficult situations. Beck found that we can learn to become aware of the negative thoughts which accompany our moods, and challenge them, rather than allow them to cause unnecessary distress.

To help you become aware of your particular negative thinking patterns, there is a 'Daily Mood Log' which you can use regularly. Version 1 of this mood log on p. 56 is designed to help you become aware of the links between your thoughts and your feelings. Version 2 of the mood log on p. 66 is a longer form designed to assist you in 'talking back' to these negative thoughts.

DAILY MOOD LOG Version 1		
Situation	Feelings	Negative automatic thoughts

Step One: Describe the Situation where You Noticed Yourself Feeling Depressed

Consider a recent situation where you became upset and perhaps stayed that way for some time afterwards. Pick a situation which is still fresh in your mind. It doesn't have to be one of the most upsetting events in your life. It's actually easier to pick a mildly upsetting event, rather than something too traumatic, to ease yourself in to this exercise.

Be as specific and as concrete as you can. In column 1, under 'Situation', record when it happened, *where* you were, *what* you were doing, *who* you were with, at the time you became upset. You might write down something like: 'Thursday, 10.05 p.m., alone at home, got a phone call from Barbara, and immediately after noticed I was upset.' Being specific about the precise situation that upset you will help you stay focused throughout this exercise when you attempt to recapture your feelings and thoughts.

Sometimes it's hard to pinpoint a precise external event which triggered your mood. For example, you might simply be sitting reading the newspaper when you suddenly notice yourself feeling quite low. Nothing that you were reading or that was going on around you seemed to provoke this. This kind of 'out of the blue' experience is very common. The explanation for it will become clearer to you when we consider what thoughts or images were passing through your mind at the time. For the moment just make a note of where you were when you started to feel down, and if you can remember being preoccupied with some particular issue, add 'thinking about X'.

Step Two: Identify the Different Feelings that Form Part of Your Mood

To understand your negative reactions to certain kinds of situations it is important to identify more precisely what feelings were triggered in those situations. While you may be very clear about having felt upset, it may take you some time to pinpoint what different kinds of feelings contributed to this sense of being 'upset'.

To help you name your feelings, try remembering how your body felt at the time. Where in your body did you notice you were upset? What did this sensation feel like? It can also be helpful to close your eyes and recall the situation in as much detail as possible: who else was present? what else was going on around you? For example, John recalled feeling upset at home one evening, but it took some time for him to realise that he was watching a film which portrayed a situation that was a mirror image of his own unhappy marriage, and his upset had been provoked. Identifying and recalling the situation in a detailed way makes it much easier to recapture the different feelings that were triggered.

Listed below are feelings which are very commonly reported by people who feel depressed. See if any of the words listed 'fit' with what you felt at the time on the occasions you were upset. Don't feel limited by this list. Feel free to use any other words that describe uniquely how you felt in such a situation.

LIST OF COMMON NEGATIVE FEELINGS

Sad	Anxious	Ashamed	Irritated	Lonely
Depressed	Frightened	Embarrassed	Frustrated	Insecure
Hurt	Nervous	Exposed	Edgy	Abandoned
Hopeless	Agitated	Guilty	Angry	Lost
Heartbroken	Panicky	Humiliated	Mad	Rejected

The difficulty most often experienced in completing this form is separating thoughts and feelings. This is because they are so closely connected in our experience. We separate them because it makes it much easier to understand our reactions and to see what requires attention if we are to change the way we feel. A simple rule of thumb is that feelings are felt in the body and they can generally be described in one word. If it takes more than one word to describe a feeling it may be that you're describing a thought. Thoughts are the spontaneous words, memories or visual images that pass through our mind when we react to something.

Step Three: Identify Your Negative Automatic Thoughts

Column 3 invites you to record your 'negative automatic thoughts' (NATs). These are the thoughts that occur spontaneously in response to some event. They are described as 'automatic' because they seem to just happen, without any particular deliberation or reflection on your part. They may take the form of specific statements, things you might say to yourself spontaneously in response to some event, e.g. 'Oh God, this is terrible!', 'I can't possibly handle this,' 'I'm no good at dealing with this kind of situation,' 'It's my own fault, I should have been able to avoid this happening.' These automatic thoughts may also take the form of fleeting images or fragments of memories which are triggered by the situation and which are associated with specific kinds of feelings. It can take time to realise what exactly it was that passed through our minds when we became upset, but being able to do so can make sense of our reactions and help us to feel less bewildered and out of control.

Recovery from depression for Sarah involved keeping a record of her thoughts and moods and gradually learning to talk back to them. The following journal entry (excerpt 6) describes what she discovered on one occasion during her hospitalisation when she became upset. It happened during one of our therapy sessions when she realised she was really thirsty and needed a drink. The particular medication she was taking had made her mouth very dry and it was becoming difficult for her to keep talking. However, she was afraid to ask if she could leave to get some water and sat for thirty minutes in session before admitting her need. When eventually she did ask to leave for a moment, she stood up and exclaimed, 'My God, I've actually asked for something!' It was a significant moment for her and I asked her to make a note of her thoughts and feelings as she sat for those thirty minutes, afraid to make her request. This is what she wrote.

Sarah's Recovery Journal
Excerpt 6

Situation	Feelings	Negative automatic thoughts
Tuesday, 12.30 p.m. During therapy session with TB I wanted to leave the session for a moment to get a drink of water, but I was too afraid to ask.	scared ashamed selfish insecure	1. I'm annoying somebody when I don't really need to. 2. I'm being demanding. 3. TB will resent me for not anticipating that I'd need water during the session. 4. He'll think I'm stupid. 5. He'll see me as worthless and not want to work with me any more. 6. If I ask for what I need I may lose whatever little I'm getting.

In completing this exercise Sarah was surprised to discover that the many different feelings she described were related to negative thoughts that she was having at the time. Just being able to write down the above made her feel a little better because her experience of being upset then made sense to her. It was not surprising that she felt 'scared' when she realised that she was frightened I would react negatively to her wanting a drink, and that, in her mind, I might decide she wasn't worth taking seriously. Writing down her thoughts also revealed one of her deeper beliefs, one of her rules of living which she hadn't realised played such an important role in her interactions with others — 'If I ask for what I need I may lose whatever little I'm getting.' This was the thought we gave most attention to when discussing her mood log as it explained much of her behaviour on the ward, i.e. not talking much to the staff, always seeming to be in good form even when she was miserable, her apparent indifference to others when they asked if she needed anything.

It is important to attend to negative thinking that is activated when we become depressed, because these thoughts intensify our mood, disable us from taking constructive action, and lower our self-esteem. The antidote for negative thinking is not simply to force ourselves to 'think positively'. You need to examine these negative thoughts, perhaps understand where they are coming from in relation to your particular life experience, and find alternative ways of thinking that are realistic and fair to yourself and others.

Talking Back to Your Negative Thoughts

As you read over Sarah's negative thoughts you may notice certain characteristics they have in common with your own when you become upset. They always place you in the worst light possible, e.g. 'I'm annoying somebody, I'm being demanding,' they usually assume the worst as far as other people are concerned, e.g. 'He'll think me stupid . . .' and they present a picture of the world where things will almost certainly get worse, e.g. 'TB will see me as worthless and not want to work with me any more.'

It is characteristic of depression that our thinking becomes distorted or biased in these ways. We blame and criticise ourselves relentlessly (**personalisation**); we assume we can read the minds of others (**mind-reading**), and we imagine others are as rejecting of us as we are of ourselves; we demand perfection of ourselves and anything less is regarded as a complete failure (**all-or-nothing** thinking); we are completely unforgiving of ourselves and insist that we should be able to be strong and capable all of the time (**should**); we interpret one setback, or one bad day, as a sign of endless defeat (**overgeneralisation**); we tend to disregard what good we have done on any one day and dwell on what didn't work out (**discounting the positive**); and we frighten ourselves by thinking of the future only in terms of the worst that could happen rather than in terms of anything positive that could happen (**catastrophisation**). These distortions are described in greater detail by David Burns in *The Feeling Good Handbook* and by Paul Gilbert in *Overcoming Depression* (see pp 107–8).

While you may identify many negative thoughts, you may find, as in Sarah's experience, that there is one particular thought that is key to your negative mood, and that when you've tackled this the others lose their power.

Below is an example of an exercise which Ann, a student nurse, completed one week before her final exams when she found herself becoming increasingly upset and unable to concentrate. She identified her negative thoughts and the main distortions that characterised these thoughts. This gave her enough relief and clarity of mind to construct a more helpful response and to focus on her work.

To challenge your negative thoughts, you might ask yourself the questions, 'What would I say to a good friend who had a similar problem?' 'Would I be as critical and negative with them if they were in a similar situation?' You might also find it helpful to consider what a good friend might say to you. Can you picture them there beside you being encouraging and supportive? What are they saying to you, and how are they saying it?

You may be mind-reading what other people are thinking and need to check this out by asking: 'What evidence do I really have for believing that X doesn't respect me?' 'Do I really know this to be true?' 'Might there be some other way of thinking about this situation?'

TALKING BACK TO NEGATIVE THOUGHTS: DEALING WITH EXAM STRESS		
Negative thoughts	Distortion	More helpful response
I shouldn't feel this way	*Should*	*It would be nice if I felt better, but feeling stressed before exams is not surprising. Being ashamed and resentful of my feelings only adds to my problems.*
I'm stupid, I always make mistakes	*Discounting the positive*	*I'm human, not stupid; and 'even I' make mistakes! I also have done some things really well on this course.*
I have too much to do — I can't manage — I'll mess up this exam and never finish this course.	*Catastrophising*	*I'm just frightening myself by thinking this way. I'd do a lot better to write out what I can achieve today and get on with it.*

One of the main goals of cognitive therapy is to empower you to take care of your self-esteem and not allow yourself to be bullied into helplessness and defeatism by your distorted negative thinking. This takes practice and you will notice how easy it is at times to slip into old negative habits. But by writing down your thoughts and talking back to them, you will be able to prevent yourself from falling foul of your mental bully.

Gradually, you learn to **become kinder to yourself**. You will learn to be encouraging of your efforts to cope with life:

I'm doing OK, this isn't easy for me but I'm hanging in, I'm getting there.

Rather than jump to negative conclusions, you stop and **check things out**. You ask:

> *Now what can I do to check if this is really true before assuming the worst and getting myself all worked up.*

If something goes wrong you **don't assume it's all your fault**:

> *OK, so this didn't quite work. I wonder why. It actually had very little to do with what I did. What are the different things that could have contributed to this not working?*

You stop assuming that you can read minds, and you **ask others what they think**:

> *I actually don't know how Mary feels about my being depressed. Maybe I could ask her and find out.*

Summary

1. How we think about ourselves or a specific crisis we are facing can determine how we feel.
2. When we are depressed our thinking becomes negative and distorted.
3. Negative thinking lowers our self-esteem, makes us suspicious of others, and disables us from dealing effectively with problems that require our attention.
4. It is possible to become aware of particular negative thoughts that upset us and learn to talk back to them.
5. As we learn to think in kinder and more optimistic ways about ourselves our self-confidence rises and we become able to tackle problems with energy and creativity.

Self-help Exercise

On page 66 there is a more complete version of the Daily Mood Log, which includes a fourth column for writing a more helpful/realistic/optimistic response to your negative thoughts. Complete the first three columns as before and then read the questions at the bottom of the page to help you construct an alternative way of looking at the situation. As you practise writing out your thoughts and talking back to them you will find that it is possible to do this very quickly in your head when you notice yourself becoming upset.

Message in a bottle

Recovery takes a step forward each time we become aware of negative, distorted thoughts, and find a more compassionate way of talking to ourselves.

DAILY MOOD LOG Version 2			
Situation	Feelings	Negative automatic thoughts	Alternative/more helpful ways of thinking

Key questions to help you construct an alternative response to a negative thought:

1. What would you say to a friend who was in the same predicament? What might a friend say to you?
2. Do you really know this is true; could there be some way you could check the evidence?
3. Can you see any way in which your thinking may be distorted?
4. What may be a fairer and more realistic way of thinking?

CHAPTER 7

Changing your Self-image

A positive self-image is our best protection against depression. When we believe in ourselves, we have the confidence to confront challenges and difficulties that come our way, and we are not afraid to seek support when we need it. We recognise our strengths, accept our limitations, and we set goals and objectives for ourselves that are realistic and attainable. There is an old adage which reads 'You can't outperform your self-image.' Our self-image defines what we believe we are capable of achieving and what we feel we can ask and expect of life.

People prone to depression generally have a very poor image of themselves. Perhaps as a result of particular negative childhood experiences they harbour painful insecurities which generally concern how 'lovable' they are, or how 'competent' they are as individuals. Depression is sparked when these self-doubts are activated and dominate their thinking. Negative thoughts and self-defeating behaviours are then set in motion, locking them into a vicious cycle and provoking feelings of being trapped, sad and lonely. The pain they feel convinces them that something indeed must be wrong with them, that they are indeed 'a failure' in some fundamental way.

People who are prone to depression often feel it is not safe or acceptable for them to 'be themselves'. Because they believe they are flawed, bad, or lacking in some way, they try hard to become what they think will make them 'acceptable' to others. They cultivate what might be described as a 'survival' personality and this can work some of the time to help them secure a sense of belonging with others. If they heard repeatedly as a child that they were 'bad' for whatever reason, they may make a strenuous effort to be 'good' all the time, to 'always do the right thing'; if they learned that being 'dependent' or emotionally needy was unacceptable, they may try hard to disown their own emotional needs, and develop an outwardly 'independent, self-reliant' personality, hiding their needs from others. Alternatively, they may become very sensitive to other people's pain and seek to care for them rather than themselves.

Because they have been in the sufferer's mind for so long, and because they often were formed in early life after repeated experiences with key people in their lives — parents, siblings, grandparents — these core beliefs are hard to change. They seem to the sufferer to be completely true, and to change them would seem somehow to be 'wrong'. They usually become the focus of psychotherapy after the sufferer has recovered from the more intense symptoms of their depression, when they feel strong enough to re-examine these survival strategies that have been so fundamental to their lifestyle. This chapter will describe some of the beliefs that may make us vulnerable to depression, and how modifying them can help sufferers achieve a lasting recovery.

I Am a Rock

If you have never felt loved for just being yourself, you may do whatever you imagine it takes to achieve a sense of belonging with others. Alternatively, you may try to convince yourself that other people's acceptance does not matter at all and distance yourself from them. You act independently, rely completely on yourself, devote lots of energy to various 'projects' and keep hidden from others any inner distress you experience. You may feel an emptiness in yourself but you battle on until the pain of chronic loneliness gives way to depression.

Richard was a man in his mid-forties who had set up his own company and developed it successfully over a number of years. He was single and had never been able to establish a close bond with anyone. He had suffered a number of bouts of depression in his life following the death of a close sibling but he had never spoken about the effect this loss had had on him. He relied on 'self-medicating' himself with alcohol to get through his black periods.

In spite of his inner torment he managed to 'keep up appearances' on the outside, because he had grown up believing that weakness of any kind was despicable. This was a belief he had 'come by honestly' at home where people with any kind of disability were viewed with contempt. After several episodes of depression he began to feel too exhausted to go it alone any more. Late one evening he came to a clear decision that he would end his suffering once and for all. He took a can of petrol to an isolated location and in the early hours of a bleak morning, he set himself on fire. By a sheer coincidence there was a farmer passing in a nearby field who spotted rising smoke and came to his assistance. He was rushed to a local burns unit and spent several months recovering, both physically and emotionally.

No one had any idea that Richard had been in such despair. He spoke of how he had managed 'to live two parallel lives' in the previous year, one where he was social and competent in his interactions with others, the other where he gradually slipped into a chronic sense of loneliness and hopelessness. When he was resuscitated in hospital he was not pleased initially. This view changed when he was able to be honest for the first time about his experience with his family and friends, who were more accepting and supportive than he had ever imagined. When he was close to discharge and had worked through many of the issues that had distressed him, he said that he was grateful in many ways for the fire because it had 'burned away' the façade of his social personality, which had only served to cut him off from others all his life. The fire exposed what was inside him to others and he discovered resources of love and support which had been unavailable to him due to his self-imposed isolation.

Each of us to some extent lives two lives, an inner life and an outer life. It is important that we can exercise our personal boundaries and keep certain things to ourselves. Privacy is one of our rights and it is important that we know this. However, when the gap between our inner life and our outer life becomes too great, we can sense a strain which is a warning sign that all may not be well. Excessive secrecy can lead to a breakdown of communication between our inner selves and others. We deprive ourselves of nurturing which is vital. Lacking a genuine connection with others we can begin to feel as if we are dying inside. We are no longer living but simply existing, relying on our social personality to mask our pain. This living is only half-living and becomes a personal hell.

A therapeutic relationship with a counsellor in whom we can confide and trust can be a crucial step for restoring a life-line between our inner experience and other people. It can allow us engage in a journey where we recover our voice and ease back the curtains we've drawn around us. As we speak and trust in another we begin to hear our own truth. Shafts of light enter our inner world. At first the light hurts our eyes but gradually we recover the ability to see colour and texture where before was only dreary monotony.

Dialogue enables us to see more clearly and face the fears and self-doubts that plague us. Gradually, we notice recurring patterns of behaviour that are obviously self-defeating and stagnant. Dialogue allows us to understand where these patterns stem from and gives us the strength to change them. As we change these patterns we make new choices that alter the course of our lives. A relationship with a therapist can be one way of making that journey from isolation to trust. Initially, it is an experience of becoming tremendously vulnerable, but over time the trust and security that one finds with a therapist can make it much easier to be open with others.

WHAT CAN WE LEARN FROM RICHARD'S STORY?

- Excessive secrecy and shame lead to isolation which is the soil upon which your depression takes root.
- Finding someone in whom we place our trust helps loosen the grip of depression.
- Never underestimate the support which people can offer.
- Recovery for depression is a journey from isolation to trusting others.

My Needs Don't Matter, Other People Are More Important than Me

Some depression-prone people have a self-image which regards their own needs as unimportant, and subordinate their lives to meeting others' expectations of them. There are a number of childhood experiences which create this type of self-image. A child may learn that to be loved they must take care of their parent, rather than seek to be cared for. They grow up with an enhanced sensitivity to the needs of those around them and they feel compelled to 'look after' everyone. They become compulsive carers who are often applauded for their endless generosity and readiness to help. However, if the tendency to overcare for others and disown one's personal needs is not addressed, the individual becomes prone to burn-out. They may continue to give but they resent that others take their availability so much for granted. At some point the inner build-up of frustration may explode, much to the shock of family, friends and co-workers who have never appreciated that the sufferer's need of love and support is as great as their apparent readiness to be there for other people. Mental health is about finding a way of relating to others that is fair, based on 'give and take'. Too much giving can leave us vulnerable to depression.

Another reason why a person may overcare for others is the fear of causing distress in others and being blamed for this. Sarah described how she had always felt afraid of causing upset in her childhood, and subsequently became overconcerned with looking after the needs of others and disowning her own. In the last chapter we noted some of Sarah's negative thoughts associated with her fear of asking for a drink of water during her therapy session. We explored some childhood experiences which gave rise to this fear, and she became aware of a general style of relating to others which had developed as a result of these experiences.

Sarah's Recovery Journal

Excerpt 7

My Image of Myself as a Child

I believed I was 'good', but I had to be really careful not to be 'bold'. I tried to help everyone and be nice because otherwise someone would get annoyed and Mammy would start to cry and it would all turn horrible. I learned to be quiet, understanding, and as kind as possible because otherwise something would go wrong and they wouldn't like me, and I'd feel awful, and upset, and really lonely. I needed to feel loved and cared for, not neglected. But it seemed that their love was conditional. I had to work hard for their love and now I feel this with everyone.

Fear of upsetting others turned to a fear of asking for what she needed and the sense that even if she did she would not be heard.

Sarah's Recovery Journal
Excerpt 8

My Self-image as an Adult

I can't seem to ask for what I need. I'm afraid to and don't. The feeling of being afraid goes back a long way. I remember as a child coming downstairs from my bedroom, late at night, and standing for ages outside the kitchen door. I wanted a glass of water but I was terrified to go through the door and ask. I don't know why I found it so hard. I think I was terrified of being given out to and told to get back to bed immediately. That it was too late for me to be up and that I had no business to be in the kitchen. In many different ways I made efforts to ask for what I wanted but it often didn't get a favourable response. Many times over the course of my life I remember saying to myself, 'I'll make an effort to say what I want but if it doesn't work, I'll never try again.' And at some point I simply gave up trying.

When you've lived for years believing that you have no fundamental right to have your needs met you stop listening to your needs and you gradually disown them. You may conclude that there is something wrong or shameful about what you are asking, and so you always put your needs second to those of others. Sarah learned that by ignoring her own needs and taking care of other people's she could earn a place in their affections. While she was in hospital she was 'the model patient' who took care of many of the older people on the ward. The nurses regarded her kindness and helpfulness to others as evidence of a strong recovery but Sarah recognised herself how 'unhealthy' such behaviour was.

Sarah's Recovery Journal

Excerpt 9

I'm now realising that when I spend all my time caring for and helping other patients, I'm actually isolating myself, disconnecting from myself, and devoting my time and attention to others rather than myself. I need to learn how to care for myself as well as other people. I need to listen to myself. I have to listen to my pain and not just that of other people. And I have to struggle with the pain inside me to try to release some of it bit by bit.

Towards the end of her stay in hospital Sarah began to change her pattern of relating to others. In the early part of her stay she had communicated little of what she needed to the nursing staff and silently resented that they seemed so insensitive to what was going on for her. However, as she began to communicate more clearly what she needed she was surprised to find just how supportive they were. She also learned to take care of her personal boundaries in a more appropriate way and not feel that she had to be completely open and compliant in relation to other people's requests. When a visiting relative asked some personal questions which Sarah found invasive, she calmly said she'd rather not talk about the issue. This was a significant shift for Sarah and it made her feel uneasy and a little guilty. With time, however, she felt stronger and clearer about asking for what she needed and giving herself permission to protect her personal boundaries.

WHAT CAN WE LEARN FROM SARAH'S STORY?

- We each have a need to belong.
- Our childhood experiences teach each of us what to do to secure a sense of acceptance and belonging. Some of what we learn can end up hurting us as adults.
- Relationships are about give and take. My needs as well as those of others deserve to be respected.
- It is not wrong to be open with others about what you need. It helps them to know you better and creates the possibility of genuine friendship.

I'm Not Good Enough

David had been very loved but overprotected all his life. He was bullied in school and it had the effect of making him feel he wasn't as good as his peers. As a result he feared any kind of competition which might expose his imagined 'incompetence'. His adolescence was marked by very happy memories of summer holidays, where he could 'play' without any pressure to compete and enjoy the easy company of friends, and very frightening memories of school, where he lived in fear of any kind of exams. He barely graduated school and took on a variety of third-level courses which he left without completing. By his mid-twenties he was unemployed, untrained and lacking any sense of direction as to how he might secure a livelihood. Repeated failures to complete any course of training had gradually eroded all his self-confidence and resulted in severe depression.

Recovery for David involved building a positive self-image. He secured part-time employment, completed two of his unfinished courses and several other certificate courses over the coming year. Each exam provoked tremendous fear and distress for him. He never believed he could pass and feared that the experience of yet another failure would be unbearably painful.

He panicked in my office before each test and pleaded to be let off the hook. He tried to convince himself that each examination was unimportant and that he would be better off finding some other less demanding project. His lifelong protection against possible failure had been to run, but together we managed to enable him to accept his fear of failure and confront it. His confidence grew with each success and carried him through the setbacks he also experienced. One year after his recovery he dropped by to tell me he was off to the Far East to take up an exciting job opportunity. He commented how he occasionally lapsed into self-criticism for all the years he had 'lost', but never for too long:

> I realise I wasted that time because I lacked self-confidence. I can do nothing about the past, but I can learn from it. I know how running away only reinforced my belief that I was incapable. I have learned how I need to act in ways that build up my self-confidence — by not running from challenges, by accepting there will be failures and setbacks. Rather than fear failure I now say to myself, 'If you're not failing, you're not learning.' And I've stopped looking for the instant fix. I accept that it takes time to build a sense of achievement.

David's self-image had been that he was essentially incompetent and he constructed a lifestyle around avoiding situations which might expose this. Exams triggered this vulnerability in him and made him anxious and depressed. His recovery required a lot of courage because he had to let go of his key survival strategy — 'Avoid failure at all costs because it will be unbearable.' By confronting his greatest fear — that he was incompetent — he discovered he was both intelligent and courageous.

WHAT CAN WE LEARN FROM DAVID'S STORY?

- You can't outperform your own self-image.
- Running from your fears only keeps alive your insecurities about yourself.
- These insecurities are triggered in key situations and make you vulnerable to depression.
- Facing your fears takes courage, but conquering them feels wonderful.

Learning to Care for What Is Most Vulnerable in You

The insecurities you have about yourself never go away completely. What changes is your ability to understand and accept these vulnerabilities and not be drawn into believing they truly represent who you are. You become aware of what situations can stir up these fears about yourself and you learn to be tender with yourself in those moments when your confidence is shaken. You are much more than your depression and you gradually learn to separate your sense of yourself from these negative patterns.

Alan was a man in his late thirties whose childhood was marked by such obscenities as his mother dressing him in girls' underwear and then exposing this when he was at play with his friends. He was constantly humiliated, told he was 'bad', and sent to school with a sense that it was a waste of time because he was 'stupid'. He worked hard to prove his mother was wrong. But at times he reverted to believing that he was 'bad' and that he had achieved very little in his life compared to his friends. This belief triggered several episodes of depression over many years. Treatment finally helped him to recover a stronger sense of self-esteem — to see himself as a young boy who had survived unbelievable abuse and who had still managed to grow into an adult capable of loving others.

He described something he did to make peace with one of the more painful memories of his childhood. The journey from home to school each morning had been especially difficult for him. He would leave home having endured a tirade of abuse, with his homework incomplete, and terrified of what further criticisms he might receive during the day. As an adult who was now recovering from depression, he realised that part of him was still that little boy who needed encouragement and support. One morning he went to the gate of his family home at the exact time that he would have left for school, and he walked the journey from home to school imagining himself in the company of this little boy. As he walked he spoke to this little boy. He told him how proud he was of him and how unfair it was that he was sent out into life so unprepared and unsupported by his parents. He promised he would always be there for him from now on and affirmed how much he believed in him and how special he was for continuing to fight through all those years when things were so dark.

Self-esteem comes down to the unique way in which we relate to ourselves, the way that we 'talk' to ourselves. It's so easy to speak with the voice of contempt, self-criticism and rejection. Recovery shifts gear when you become able to accept yourself as you truly are, with all your vulnerabilities and frailties. As you take some pressure off yourself to be other than you are, and acknowledge where you need nurturing and encouragement to grow, you will find an ease with yourself that is new and refreshing.

Summary

We remain vulnerable to depression as long as we hold destructive beliefs about ourselves and continue to relate to other people in ways that do not allow us to genuinely connect with them. To be ourselves with others is a goal worth pursuing because it frees us from a lot of needless pressure and frustration, and opens up possibilities for lasting friendship and intimacy. But this takes time and repeated effort. To be ourselves is as much a gift from others as it is a choice that we make. Success depends on finding people we can trust, who allow us to be ourselves.

Self-help Exercise

Consider the following questions and give yourself time to answer them.

- What were some of the important messages you picked up from your family about how to survive in this world?
- In what ways have these messages helped you — how have they made you **strong**? In what ways have they set you up for certain kinds of problems — how have they made you **vulnerable**?
- What messages or rules of living do you need to change to leave you less vulnerable to depression?
- Can you see any way you might ease up on some of these rules that would make living a gentler experience for you?

Message in a bottle

Recovery means refusing to buy into rules of living that no longer serve us, and trying new ways of relating to ourselves and others.

CHAPTER 8

Putting it All Together: Tom's Story

One Sunday, an hour after returning from coaching the junior football team, Tom had his 'heart attack'. His GP was summoned and, finding him collapsed on the dining room floor with an alarmingly low pulse, dispatched him by ambulance to the local Accident and Emergency. Relatives were contacted 'just in case' and gathered around the cardiac monitor. Their respectful silence and concerned faces spoke volumes. Tom got the message: he was forty-three, happily married with five children, he had a good job, but his number was up. How would they cope after he was gone?

It was no comfort to Tom when the suspected 'heart attack' was ruled out and the much more benign condition of pericarditis diagnosed. In five days he was treated and discharged but what followed was six years of chronic depression. Two ten-week psychiatric admissions, ECT and drug treatment did little to help. When he eventually was referred for cognitive therapy those years of relentless misery had taken their toll. He didn't feel much like talking.

Tom was slight in stature and spoke in a way that was direct and honest. He sat in my office and seemed unsure of why he was there. I was yet another in the long series of professionals he'd encountered, and by his demeanour it was clear he didn't believe I could do any more for him than others before me. The referral note from his doctor described him as a man with a negative attitude to most things in his life. He had a six-year history of depression but treatment had been unable to shift his pessimism.

Tom worked hard for his family and he expected little in return other than that his children would leave the family home with a self-confidence he'd always lacked. He spoke of his own father who had been particularly harsh to him and 'broke his spirit' as a young boy. He had left school and home as a young teenager and started work. By nineteen years of age he had proved himself as a successful bread salesman and a series of promotions followed which enabled him to marry and set up a home. He now worked as a salesman with a successful family business and he was a much-valued employee. His loyalty to the company was uncompromising and he worked over and above the call of duty. He had five children who adored him as much as he did them. So why had he turned away from life and lapsed into such an immovable depression?

> I didn't want to live. I just wasn't able to face living. I thought everybody could see me as I felt and what I felt in my mind was so horrifying. I couldn't bear to think that people could see me in that way. I withdrew from everything I was used to. I had no confidence in going to meet customers or to collect the debts the company was owed. I'd find myself driving up the road and having to stop and come home. I basically just wanted to sit in a room by myself and be left alone.

His condition deteriorated in the months that followed. For six years he appeared to shut himself off from the world and he felt thoroughly miserable. He remained at work but came home every evening and fell asleep in the chair after dinner. He showed no interest in activities that had been previously a source of pleasure for him, like gardening, football, being with his children and meeting friends. The family watched his decline and wondered whether they were perhaps the cause of his pain. They walked on eggshells around him, making few demands on him and trying not to discommode him. As time passed, they relied less and less on him to participate in normal family life. They stopped expecting him to be 'Dad'.

> I felt myself retreating away from the wife and children because of the fear that there was something there that they could see — 'Daddy is going mad.' They weren't saying anything like this but I felt in my mind they were saying it.

Tom's depression continued to convince him that he was worthless, incompetent and unloved. It was an enormous effort for him just to get through each day. The most painful part of it all was that his torment seemed to be endless. Not surprisingly, he began to consider whether the only way out of his pain might be death:

> I did feel that it would be the best thing for everybody if I ran the car over a cliff or ended my life in some way. But something inside me said, 'Don't be stupid,' and thank God that something stopped me.

For people who are depressed a key part of the problem is the inability on the part of others to appreciate just how demoralised and isolated they feel.

> People don't understand depression. If you have a broken arm everybody has all the pity in the world for

> you. If you have a broken leg people will help you up a stairs, open a door for you. But if you have depression, nobody knows only yourself, so you are living with it yourself. They say cancer is a killer, but depression is the worst disease out. It's a prison sentence which seems to go on for ever.

His first professional contact was with his GP, who diagnosed depression and suggested a referral to a psychiatrist for medication. At one point he was on six to eight tablets daily, but, as can happen in some cases, these did little to help him. Hospital admission was arranged on two different occasions:

> Hospitalisation didn't help me in the condition I was in. I felt I was just a number. Don't get me wrong. I know the country is full of patients. I didn't want any special kind of treatment, but what I would have loved was for somebody to come and sit beside the bed and talk to me about how I was, and what my problem was. To explain it to me. To be given tablets and left there by yourself, your meals served up, and staff dropping in to say hello and goodbye, wasn't enough for me. I wanted to know what was happening, why I felt the way I was and what the end product was going to be.

What appeared to happen in Tom's case was that his depression was viewed exclusively as a medical problem. He was perceived to have a chemical imbalance which would be corrected only by specific medications. While these helped to ease the pain of his depression, they were unable to remove the underlying causes of his problem. Electroconvulsive therapy (ECT) was also administered during his hospital admission. This is a treatment which delivers a very mild electric shock to the brain and thereby alters the brain chemistry. In cases of severe chronic depression this has been found to have dramatic benefits in lifting a sufferer's mood. However, this treatment did little to improve his situation. What was missing was any form of counselling or therapy which could have offered Tom the opportunity to understand and resolve the root causes of his problem.

Cognitive therapy believes that to understand why a person reacts badly to certain events you have to understand the meaning a particular event had for them. How we read a situation determines how we react. Tom's depression had been triggered by his becoming ill but the meaning of this experience to him had never fully been explored. This was the key to understanding why he had become so upset and how his distress had developed into clinical depression.

He described how what had troubled him the most was not actually the imagined cardiac arrest, the imminent threat of death, or the potential loss of his family, but rather a deep insecurity which had seized hold of him and maintained its grip ever since. As he lay there in those moments waiting for the ambulance to arrive he heard clearly the cutting voice of his father when he was a youngster, saying: 'You're a loser, you can never be counted on, you just don't have what it takes to make it.' Tom interpreted this crisis as proof that his dad was right. That he was unreliable, and that his family should never count on him to provide for them. His self-esteem was completely undermined as he surrendered to this verdict. He put a distance between himself and his family and when eventually they stopped counting on him, he interpreted this as proof that he had little to offer them. The following diagram illustrates the sequence of events that triggered Tom's depression and the vicious cycle of negative thinking and self-defeating behaviour which maintained it over six years.

WHAT TRIGGERED TOM'S DEPRESSION

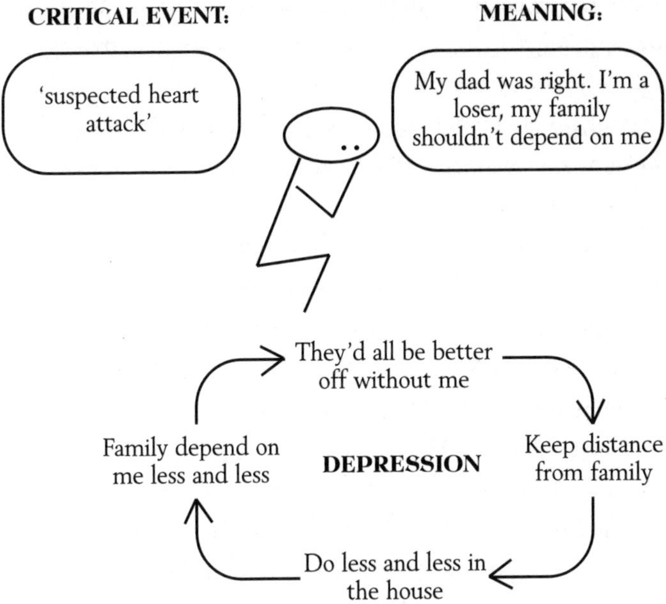
CRITICAL EVENT:
MEANING:
'suspected heart attack'
My dad was right. I'm a loser, my family shouldn't depend on me
They'd all be better off without me
Keep distance from family
Do less and less in the house
Family depend on me less and less
DEPRESSION

In our sessions together, Tom began to see how the negative view of himself he'd harboured since childhood was at the root of his depression.

> I was made feel very inferior as I was growing up . . . that I was never good enough for anything or to be anything. When the 'heart attack' came it gave what I was led to believe was more ammunition to get me down. Which it did.

He recalled a critical event that had sparked the poor relationship he'd had with his father. When he was eight years old his sister, who was aged twelve, died. In a family of eleven siblings he had never been that close to his mother, and this particular sister had been the person who mothered him. On the morning she died, his father had come into his bedroom and told him he wouldn't be going to school that day. He watched the funeral pass by through his front window and felt completely bewildered by it all. Nothing was ever the same afterwards and his relationship with his father deteriorated badly.

> It basically had to do with my dad. But then I didn't blame him either. The more I looked at things the more I realised it basically wasn't his fault. I lost a sister who was like a mother to me. My dad also lost a daughter whom he thought the world of. And I feel he looked upon me as though I should have died and my sister should have lived. So he downed me always no matter what I did. He never thought me capable of any good. I didn't dislike him, I loved him. I did everything possible to please him, but it didn't make any difference to him. He just didn't seem to relate to me at all. It was a pity really because it would have been a better life for both of us if he had realised my feelings for him. I feel he was depressed when he lost my sister but I lost as much as he lost.

Deep down he had always believed his dad was right and he had survived by adopting certain protective mechanisms to block out this image of himself as unreliable and a failure. He had always overworked to compensate for this imagined deficiency. His coping was by any standard impressive, but when he was incapacitated that Sunday afternoon he had relived, with complete conviction, the shameful self-image he had formed as a boy.

Tom continued to live out this negative belief in the six years that followed. He adopted a passive and ineffectual role at home because he believed it was in his family's best interest that they should not depend on him. In his mind this was the best he could do to avoid further experiences of letting them down, which would have been more than he could bear, and which he believed would hurt them also. For the first time he understood why he was behaving as he was in respect to those he loved most in the world.

As he recalled these formative childhood experiences the intense pain of a young eight-year-old boy, whose sister had died tragically, and whose father seemed to turn against him viciously in the years that followed, became very vivid. Despair slowly gave way to anger as he struggled against that negative inner voice he had internalised, which continued to drain his energy and his will to live.

Tom's early attempts to refute this mental 'bully' with the evidence of a life lived out steadily, faithfully and successfully were timid at best. After a number of therapy sessions he visited his sister's grave with the intention of telling her for the first time how upset he had been. However, he was unable to do this. His explanation on returning to therapy was that his father was buried next to her and he could imagine his father criticising him for being so weak. With time he became stronger and challenged the memory of all his father had said to him in anger. As he remembered the pain of his past he also recognised the strength of the bullied child within him, the child that had survived, grown into an adult and had given a good life to others. He recognised too that his dad's behaviour reflected specific problems that afflicted his dad, rather than anything he, Tom, had provoked or deserved.

As a result of trying to prove his dad wrong about him being a 'loser', he realised that he had pushed himself to live by a rule: 'If I do not provide completely for my children, then I will prove myself to be an incompetent loser.' Living rigidly by this rule left him constantly worried that anything might happen to threaten his job. As a result he worked seven days a week, hoping to establish himself as indispensable, but actually increasing the risks to his health and putting his job and his life in serious jeopardy.

While it was an immense relief for Tom to understand the root cause of his depression, the real challenge for him was to put the lie to the belief that he was unreliable. He needed to break the patterns of negative thinking and behaviour that had locked him into depression, and to rebuild his self-esteem. He started by acting differently around his family, and contributing to each of them in small ways. As he became stronger he learned to notice when his negative thinking became active in his mind, and he began to talk back to these thoughts rather than collapsing inside and assuming they were true. Eventually, he began to speak more directly to his father and counter his accusations.

> I did everything. I went to the graveyard. I discussed with him what he had wanted of me. As sure as hell if there is a heaven we're going to have a hell of a chat. I got it out into the open and had a good look at it and I saw that my negative thinking was a ghost of despair and depression. It was a voice telling me something that was completely untrue about myself. I learned to accept it was untrue and the more I did this the more courage I got to fight it. Basically, I was able to fight with him to let go of me, that I didn't deserve what he did and what he was still doing in my head. That I wasn't the type of person that he thought I was; that I was going to succeed and that he wasn't going to stop me. It was a hard struggle, because he had a terrible grip on me. If you love someone they have a grip on you. And I did love my dad. And I'd tell him that tomorrow if I met him because I still love him. But I didn't deserve what he was doing to me, because I wasn't the type of person that he had made me out to be.

Once Tom began to believe that he could be counted on, it was noticeable that his relationship with the family changed. He began to take more initiative at home and gradually he became 'Dad' again. It was hard at first for the family to adjust to his behaviour change because they were so used to seeing him as a quite passive self-centred figure. Meetings were arranged between him and his wife to discuss how he could re-enter the family, and her difficulty in trusting that his improvement would last. Her support was critical in enabling Tom to return to being a father and a husband.

As he reworked his relationships at home, Tom also related differently to others outside the home. He took more initiative with colleagues at work and with friends he'd been neglecting. His self-confidence steadily returned and his depression lifted.

> I'm better able to face things now. I'm not afraid to express how I feel to others. Before I sat back and was silent even if I didn't agree with what was being said. I would have thought that anything I had to say was stupid. Now I believe in myself and I say what I think.

As therapy drew to a close we considered the possible situations which might cause him to relapse. We discussed some practical coping skills that would carry him beyond therapy and help him for the rest of his life. In the five years that have passed since his ending therapy Tom has been in touch on occasions. He has never since experienced the despair he endured for those six bleak years of his life. He has had bad days, some very difficult life experiences, but he has coped with them without letting himself be drawn back into the grip of clinical depression.

> My routine to survive is that I go out each morning and I say to myself this day is going to be better than yesterday. No matter what problem I meet I say it's only a problem, I will deal with it. If I think it's too much for me, I walk away from it and I come back to

> it with fresh thoughts the next day. Before it would get me down and I wouldn't sleep at night. Now I see each problem as just another part of life, and tomorrow it will be better. I'm coping, I'm living, I enjoy what I want to enjoy. And I am quite happy with what I have. That's it.

As therapy draws to a close people become clearer about the elements of their life experience which contributed to their depression and at the same time they begin to see these experiences in a new way. Although the negative elements of their stories remain the same the meaning changes: painful memories are now accepted, but they are perceived as having given the sufferer unique and important sensitivities which can be important in dealing with others. This was also the case with Tom, who realised that his father's abusive behaviour had given him a vital insight in raising his own children:

> My dad really taught me how important it is to build up a person's feeling of self-confidence. The human spirit can be easily broken . . . At least my children can never say I did that to them and that's the most important thing I've ever given them. My dad gave me that. Maybe it's OK I went through what he put me through to teach me that, but maybe it's OK to stop doing that to myself now.

CHAPTER 9

Living with a Depressed Person

Living outside the wall of depression can be very difficult. Loved ones can feel as confused as the sufferer and become worn out, guilty, and exasperated by their inability to help someone about whom they deeply care. What follows are some suggestions to help you be present to the sufferer in a supportive way, while not being drawn into the darkness of their depression.

For convenience, we can think in terms of two different stages in living with this problem: the stage where neither you nor the sufferer knows what's wrong and their mood and their behaviour become steadily worse, and a further stage when they accept that there is a problem which may require some form of external help. Each stage presents unique challenges and pitfalls to the depressed person and to those close to them.

(1) Living with Someone who has Not Yet Accepted They Have a Problem

In the early stages of depression the sufferer may deny there is anything wrong and gradually cut themselves off from you and everyone else. You try everything to lift their spirits but nothing works. In moments of serious exasperation, you resort to telling them to 'cheer up' and 'snap out of it'. This only aggravates the situation even more. Confusion sets in and you come up with all kinds of explanations for what might be happening: 'Is there something wrong physically with them?' 'Is it our relationship?' 'Is it me?' 'Should we be living somewhere else?' You struggle alone with these questions, because it is not easy to talk about your concerns with somebody who is withdrawn and non-communicative. Eventually, your explanations may come down to blaming them for being 'selfish' or blaming yourself for being 'inadequate'.

The pitfalls at this stage are *isolation* and *confusion*. The isolation into which the depressed person sinks can become a powerful factor within a family. Almost without realising it, the family can become cut off from their normal social supports. Because the sufferer does not find it easy to have visitors, friends and relatives are no longer invited to drop in. Children don't invite their friends in, and neighbours don't drop by casually, as they can sense a change in the atmosphere. The most important survival strategy for you during this phase is to confide in someone about what is happening. Someone who can help you to see you are not imagining the pressures you are under, that there is indeed an issue, which both you and the sufferer have to face.

When you have achieved some clarity about what is happening, it is easier to talk to the sufferer without it becoming a mutual blaming session where nothing gets resolved. You may have to take the initiative with the sufferer and speak to them very candidly about what is happening for you at an emotional level. Be very simple and specific about how you feel. And, as far as possible, speak slowly and calmly. People who are sinking into depression find it impossible to cope with intense emotion or criticism. Try to share your own feelings, rather than blame them for what they are doing 'wrong'.

For example, saying something like:

When you sit in silence at the dinner table I feel lonely and cut off and start asking myself all kinds of questions about what I might have done wrong to upset you is a lot easier for the sufferer to hear than

> *Why are you doing this to all of us, why are you being so selfish?*

If their state of mind continues to worsen and the depressed person seems unable to acknowledge they have a problem, it may be appropriate for you to seek expert advice on how best to respond and be helpful. You could consult with your GP or some local counsellor, and discuss the problems that you are experiencing being around the sufferer. You are not blaming them, you are not seeking to betray loyalties, you are simply trying to access support that will help you stay calm and grounded. There may also be issues around how you should look after the needs of any children that may be involved, and the advice of someone with expertise in these matters may be crucial. There are many support groups for depressed people, such as Aware, and these offer helplines which you can phone for confidential advice (01 679 1711).

What one woman found hardest in this phase of her husband's depression was having to 'detach to survive'. In her mind this seemed so 'selfish' since she often walked out of the room and left him in his despair. She had to challenge one of her own beliefs, which was, 'If you really love someone, you suffer along with them no matter what it takes.' She had three children and over time she learned that 'You can't make them better and to try to means you end up sinking, and being no good to anybody.'

There is a point where relatives and close friends no longer should live through the exasperation of not knowing what is happening with somebody, and neither should they have to cope with the fear that the sufferer may do something impulsive and self-destructive. If the problem reaches a crisis point and the sufferer seems unable or unwilling to accept they need help, it may be necessary for you to step back completely and refuse to support them any further until they do. This might even involve leaving them for a period of time. You would not do this lightly, but when you no longer see any other way of communicating to them how painful the situation has become for everyone.

(2) Living with Someone who Accepts They Are Depressed

Hopefully, a time will arrive when the sufferer accepts that they do have a problem which may benefit from some direction from a specialist in the field. When this acceptance has been achieved and arrangements have been made to meet with someone, there is some lifting of tension within your relationship and your role in supporting them becomes slightly clearer for you. There are serious challenges ahead as you both negotiate this difficult time, but at least there is some hope of their breaking free of the stalemate of the past few months. The following points are suggestions which may help you to cope with this phase of their recovery.

(a) Don't be Provoked by Negative Behaviours

People who feel badly about themselves frequently act in ways that seem designed to provoke others to reject them. They become exhausted with carrying this sense of 'badness' inside themselves and they attempt to locate some of their bad feelings in those around them. Accusations are hurled at loved ones blaming them for everything that is wrong: 'It's all your fault, you never support me'; 'You never really respected me and you've always treated me as if I'm stupid.'

The most hurtful comments are often those levelled at children. One man who was known for his gentleness and sensitivity to others was given to making cruel comments to his children when he was depressed. He would tell them that he regretted ever having them and he would repeatedly threaten to get rid of them. In his recovery he would recall these comments he had made and bitterly regret them. Because they had never been balanced by him saying positive and encouraging things to his children, his relationship with them suffered badly, and it took many years to be repaired. His openness and honest apology to them when he had recovered was crucial in rebuilding this relationship. From the children's perspective, they mentioned years later that what helped them to overcome the hurt their father had inflicted was being able to separate who he was as a person from his depression.

These accusations are often spoken from a place of deep self-hate. To want to react in anger is perfectly understandable, but more often this only serves to aggravate the situation. There is a point where you simply may need to leave the room, but if you can talk back to the hurt and fear that lies behind these accusations, you may find that the sufferer's tone softens.

Thus, an unhelpful response to unreasonable accusations may be something like:

> *That's so unfair, I've always been here for you.*

While this may seem completely justified, it only fuels the fire of self-hate and anger that grips the sufferer in that moment. A more constructive response which acknowledges the confusion and pain behind the tirade may be something like:

> *It sounds as if you're feeling bad about everything including our relationship, as if there is nothing good in the world to hold on to.*

(b) Respect, Even When You Can't Understand

When you are feeling happy and clear-headed, the complaints of a depressed person seem completely unreasonable. Why would they have such a poor opinion of themselves? Don't they appreciate all they have achieved? Don't they realise how much people care about them?

The temptation is naturally to help them see everything more rationally. But someone in depression cannot easily make this shift and they can feel even more 'stupid' for not being able to 'think positively'. There is a time to fight with the negative thinking inherent in depression, but there is a time to respect that someone is severely upset and needs companionship rather than logic. Allow yourself to be with the sufferer in moments of difficulty, and take the pressure off yourself to find an immediate solution. To respect their experience rather than trying to fix it is what the sufferer most appreciates in those very dark moments.

Many black moods have to be endured for some hours or days before they ease up. When the break comes, dialogue becomes easier and there may well be a place for helping loved ones remember positive aspects of their life that have become eclipsed in depression.

(c) Give Space but Don't Isolate

People in distress need space and time to deal with their difficult moods. Having someone around who monitors their every frown only adds to their sense of being a burden. On the other hand, if they are able to feel that their upset does not always distress everybody else, this gives them time to work through the ups and downs of their recovery and 'rejoin' the company of others when they are feeling better.

For parents with young adult children going through depression, there is often a conflict about how much space to offer and how much they should check in on how their child is doing. There is a delicate balance to be achieved between giving someone a respectful amount of space and yet not isolating them within the home through complete neglect. You have to walk a difficult path between on the one hand suffocating them and on the other hand abandoning them.

Having one regular routine where you can meet and check in briefly with the sufferer may be enough to keep in touch without making constant enquiries about their mood. Such an occasion should be a time and place where each of you can feel relaxed enough to bring up difficult issues. For some it may be driving home, for others it may be after a meal when everyone has finished up and left. Find such a moment in the week that works for you as much as for them and content yourself with checking in on their progress on that particular occasion. Acknowledge whatever is still tough for them and be sure also to acknowledge small but important achievements that have been made in the previous week.

(d) Don't Wear a Worried Look around the Sufferer All the Time

The most important message you can convey to the sufferer is your faith in their ability to fight this depression and to come through it. Maybe they require some outside help, medication may be critical, but ultimately it is they who will struggle and overcome this mood. It will be their choice, and their victory, and they need to sense from you that you have that kind of belief in them. They don't need a sympathy which suffocates and unintentionally disempowers them.

You cannot take responsibility for another's life. Love sometimes requires that you let others struggle through very difficult moments without seeking to rescue or to 'mind' them too much and trusting that they will make the right choices for themselves.

(e) Keep Your Own Family and Social Life Going

Don't allow another person's depression to drain your energy and to completely disrupt your personal life. Keep in touch with your own work projects, leisure pursuits, and especially with friends that nurture and support you. Don't let go of whatever sustains you. There will be times when you will need to say to the sufferer, 'I need to leave now and give myself a break.' This may seem harsh, if they are in a difficult space, but you need time for yourself in order to be able to be there for them and the rest of the family when you return.

(f) Don't Underestimate Children who May Be Involved

Children have an uncanny way of picking up atmospheres and tensions within the home. It may be appropriate in the early stages to try to protect them from the suffering of a parent, but to continue to deny something is wrong when they clearly sense this to be the case only serves to confuse and worry them more. Children can generally cope very well with knowing someone else is unwell or upset, but they do not do at all well with feeling that they are inflicting or causing that upset for a parent. Their apparent silence and indifference to what is happening should never be taken as a sign that they are unaffected by the suffering of a parent. At some point it is best to be very honest about the fact that the sufferer is upset and feeling bad about themselves. This locates the problem where it belongs and protects children, who are inclined to blame themselves for whatever they sense is wrong in the home.

It is not uncommon for people in depression to say very cruel things to children in one of their dark moods and these types of comments need to be addressed rather than be allowed to fester in the mind of the child.

I remember seeing a family of a man who had been depressed for many years but who was refusing to continue treatment. His wife and three of his four children attended for an initial session and I remarked on the absence of the daughter who was at that time fourteen. They explained that this would be much too upsetting for her and they had arranged to meet me without her knowledge. I had not met this child but in principle I found this to be an uncomfortable arrangement so I requested that she might be brought along to the next meeting. At all subsequent meetings she turned out to be the person who most accurately portrayed the atmosphere of the home and who most sensitively could relate to her father in his different moods. Her insights guided me in helping this family and her father. It was also apparent that this young girl was trying desperately hard to make everyone else happy while suffering herself with problems of sleepwalking, bed-wetting and an inability to concentrate at school. By allowing her to be present and voice her concerns I was able to communicate to her that we would look after her dad and free her of that sole responsibility.

Summary

Depression is confusing to those who live with someone in the grip of this disorder. On the one hand it's easy to become intolerant and critical of the sufferer, and on the other hand there is the danger of becoming drawn into their experience and becoming exhausted by it. Find someone to support you and keep you grounded. Attend to your work and give yourself breaks to look forward to, which are nurturing for you. Cruel things said in the midst of rage and despair may cause deep wounds which fester long after the depression has lifted. It's important to appreciate that this was depression talking and not the person you know and love. Know how much you can tolerate and acknowledge when you've reached your limit. Discuss in a respectful way with the sufferer that they may need to get help to resolve their problems. There is only so much you can do. To try to do more wears you down to a point where you have nothing to give.

CHAPTER 10

Beyond Depression: Staying Well and Dealing with Setbacks

◆◆◆

When I was depressed, I would let myself become overstressed to a point where I either exploded or collapsed in tears at the end of a day. Now I can acknowledge when things are getting too much for me and I slow down. Instead of criticising myself for not coping as well as I imagine I should, I say to myself, 'This is a bad day, take it easy, pace yourself, deal with one problem at a time.'

◆◆◆

Recovery from depression is a journey rather than a destination. It begins when you refuse to believe that being depressed is the best you can hope for. It takes time, and there will be lots of ups and downs. It requires you to take risks, trying out new ways of living within yourself and with others. Recovery takes you beyond what is familiar and this can be frightening. It's hard to let go old patterns of thinking and acting and you may feel 'strange' or 'wrong' when you act in ways that put yourself and your own mental health first.

Recovery can take you by surprise. It can creep up on you so that you find yourself feeling a strong sense of well-being without knowing exactly where it came from. Several people have described how they felt an 'unusual' feeling for some days following months of depression. After some time they recognised that feeling as a sense of vitality which had been absent for so long.

In her book *The Drama of Being a Child* Alice Miller describes recovery as the achievement of an ease within ourselves that allows us make room for many different feelings:

> The true opposite of depression is neither gaiety nor the absence of pain, but vitality — the freedom to experience spontaneous feelings. It is part of the kaleidoscope of life that these feelings are not only happy, beautiful or good but can reflect the entire range of human experience, including envy, jealousy, rage, disgust, greed, despair and grief (p. 71).

Recovery does not mean the absence of feeling vulnerable. It means discovering a new strength in ourselves which accepts our vulnerabilities without being crushed by them. Someone who has truly recovered from depression is someone who carries within them a greater awareness of how weak they are, but also a realisation that their true self is not defined by their fragility.

Recovery doesn't eliminate your vulnerabilities; rather it changes your relationship with those aspects of your self. They are part of who you are but not all of what you are about. They stem from life experiences that have left you insecure about your own basic goodness and competence. It is possible to accept these shadows of your past and to know what kinds of situations are likely to spark them into life. It may be as simple as receiving a criticism from someone, a stressful week that leaves you exhausted, a task you can't seem to complete, or a friend who doesn't get in touch after promising to. These can hurt you more than they should, but you recognise the hurt in you that they awaken and you learn to live gently with your own reactions.

A formula which is simple to remember may help you acknowledge when you become upset while preventing you from slipping back into depression. Think of this as the AAA relapse prevention plan:

THE AAA RELAPSE PREVENTION PLAN	
Aware	Know where your vulnerabilities lie and learn to notice how easily they can be sparked into life.
Accept	Accept how you feel without being dismayed or disappointed by your reaction.
Action	Think about what you've learned in your recovery and consider what you need to do in this crisis to take care of yourself. Then do it!

Taking action to respond to a crisis so that you don't lapse into depression may involve adopting a number of different strategies depending on the situation with which you are confronted. For example, if you find yourself becoming distressed when you are alone, it may be you need to contact a friend. The availability of a support group such as Aware or the Samaritans may provide such a lifeline. If your upset is over a task which seems to be overwhelming, consider breaking down the task into small steps and dealing with one at a time. The table below summarises some of the strategies which have been described earlier in this book and which might be helpful in relation to the particular crisis you face.

KEY POINTS TO HELP YOU IN YOUR RECOVERY

Relating to yourself in a new way:

- Remember what worked for you in the past when you feel upset.
- Remind yourself that your moods change and that you rarely stay 'down' for too long.
- Do something rather than do nothing.
- Give yourself credit for what you have achieved today, no matter how tiny that was.
- Watch out for negative thoughts and don't let them bully you.
- Be compassionate with yourself when things don't work out as you hoped.

Relating to others in a new way:

- Be open about how you feel with someone you can trust.
- Assert your needs with family, with friends and at work.
- Avoid blaming yourself for other people's problems.
- Take care of your personal boundaries: the space you need for yourself, the issues you wish to keep private from others.
- Don't be pressured into giving in to unreasonable requests.

Having Something to Hold On To in a Crisis

In your moments of pain you will need something to hold on to to get you through. This might be literally a physical object that gives you comfort: an object that holds some good memories for you, a photograph of someone who loves you, a gift which reminds you of what you have meant to others. Or it may even be a phrase someone spoke to you and which made you feel calm. Perhaps they recognised you in your pain and said something simple like 'Trust yourself, you can come through this.'

Having a person you can talk to in difficult moments can be of immeasurable help. It may be wise to ask them if you can turn to them if the going gets rough. Agreeing with them ahead of time that you will contact them in a crisis makes it more likely that you will. If you are prone to depression, it's too easy to convince yourself that nobody would want to hear from you, and let yourself withdraw into a tormented loneliness.

A positive sense of what you want to achieve in your life may be what you can hold on to in a crisis. It can help to set down some of your life objectives as you emerge from depression. The crisis of depression may have shifted some of your goals, and shown you more clearly what are the most important, the most valued aspects of your life. To stay well you may need to reorder your values. Approval from others at any price may not seem so attractive any more; being in control, being right, winning in every situation, may suddenly seem vain and meaningless. Having these as your most important values can cut you off from others and force you to be something you are not. Take time to set yourself some personal objectives for the coming year. What would be important for you to put in place in your life in the coming year; what would you like to achieve in your work, your personal relationships, your hobbies, and in your family? By taking time to clarify these objectives, you clarify what is most important in your life, what really matters to you, what you can 'hold on to' through the coming year.

Summary

Maturity and inner strength do not mean being on top of things all the time, or feeling good all the time. Strength is about being able to accept how you are feeling at any point in time, including all those times you feel down, and deal with it in a way that is accepting, compassionate and encouraging. Recovery is about becoming more open with yourself, more spontaneous, and accepting all the different aspects of your personality. The key is learning to live gently with yourself and knowing what you have to hold on to that matters in a moment of crisis. Recovery is about allowing ourselves to be human, and not expecting something superhuman of ourselves.

This book has tried to reach you in the midst of your confusion and pain and offer some understanding and guidance. It has never tried to minimise your pain or make recovery sound like something simple. What have been suggested by way of self-help strategies are based on treatment programmes for depression that have been found to work. By describing a wide range of recovery strategies it hopefully has offered some which are directly applicable to your personal situation.

To conclude, I would like to quote for the last time from Sarah's journal. After a difficult struggle with depression for over a year, she recovered a strong sense of herself and felt happier in herself than she had ever remembered. This positive feeling has persisted and she is gradually rebuilding her life. Her recovery involved all the strategies I have described in this book, and the support of family and friends. Medication was an important aspect of her recovery in stabilising her mood. Therapy brought her to look at the roots of her negative self-image, to find an ease within herself and to learn to like herself again. Like many people, Sarah's honesty with herself and her courage to persist through the confusion were an inspiration to all who had the privilege of assisting in her journey.

Sarah's Recovery Journal

Excerpt 10

Recovery takes time. It takes all the time you've got. It starts when you realise that you are depressed and you are willing to change how you feel. And it's that will that keeps you going. It vanishes every so often, but reappears so gently at times and so strong at others because you really want to be you. You want to be the hidden you, who secretly you know is wonderful, but who you're afraid to be in case it doesn't work out. But it's taking those risks and allowing yourself time that gets you there. It's not easy to fight with the thoughts that keep you chained to depression. It's a long and difficult struggle, but it's worth while.

I won't ever say I'm glad to have experienced depression, but I wouldn't know what I know now if I hadn't gone through it. I've come a long way from some very dark moments and from painful days of despair. The pain doesn't completely vanish, it eases and it lessens as you start to understand it.

I always had a feeling that there was something special in me, I always suspected it. And now I'm beginning to see what that special thing is. It's me, it's being me. It's being Sarah as she's never been before. It's feeling what I feel and understanding my feelings. Most of all it's the beginning of caring about me and looking after myself and allowing myself to do so.

And there are times throughout the day when I feel a warmth inside me for what seems like no apparent reason. It's these moments which are so precious for me, when I feel happy, relaxed and content as I realise just how precious life is. I'm glad to be alive!

Self-help Books: A Guided Review

The following review of self-help literature on depression highlights a small selection of the many books that are available on this subject.

The Feeling Good Handbook, Dr David D. Burns (Plume/ Penguin, 1990)

This is the sequel to David Burns's best-seller on depression, *Feeling Good*. The earlier book described a cognitive therapy approach to depression, and was notable for its enthusiasm. The later *Handbook* was written to explain more clearly to the reader how to apply these techniques to their particular problems.

The Depression Workbook: A Guide for Living with Depression and Manic Depression, Mary Ellen Copeland (New Harbinger Publications, 1992)

This workbook is the result of a study made by the author of the coping strategies and experiences of 120 depressives and manic depressives, and also draws very explicitly on what Mary Copeland learned from her own struggles with these difficulties. It is a series of exercises dealing with such issues as understanding depression, setting goals, accessing the support you need, changing your lifestyle so that it promotes wellness, learning new ways of thinking.

Overcoming Depression, Paul Gilbert (Robinson Publications, 1997)

This book provides a more in-depth exploration of depression and how it is to be overcome than either of the above. It is written with great sensitivity and describes in some detail when and how medication might be important, the social as well as psychological causes of depression.

The Drama of Being a Child, Alice Miller (Virago Press, 1997)
This is a book to be read when one is well on the road to recovery and is interested in exploring the possible childhood origins of their depression, and strong enough to do so.

Breaking the Bonds, Dorothy Rowe (HarperCollins, 1994)
Dorothy Rowe's earlier book *Depression — The Way Out of Your Prison* was a classic text which was often recommended by therapists dealing with depression. She writes with a tremendous empathy for the sufferer, and pinpoints some key beliefs and values which serve to maintain depression.

Manage Your Mind: The Mental Fitness Guide, Gillian Butler and Tony Hope (Oxford University Press, 1998)
This is a wonderfully written book covering all aspects of staying mentally healthy and building up your self-confidence. It draws together the best of psychological research to show how problems of daily living including depression and anxiety can be tackled.

Malignant Sadness, Lewis Wolpert (Faber and Faber, 1999)
This book is perhaps the most personal of all mentioned in this short review. It provides an excellent short account of all the various approaches to depression and discusses most informatively and clearly the biological understanding of depression and the importance of medication.

Coping with Depression and Elation, Dr Patrick McKeon (Sheldon Press, 1995)
This book presents practical ways to cope with depression and manic depression. It is particularly useful in describing different types of mood swings and how they can best be treated.

Useful Addresses

Ireland

Al-Anon
5 Capel Street, Dublin 1. Tel. 01 873 2699.

Alcoholics Anonymous
109 South Circular Road, Leonard's Corner, Dublin 8.
Tel. 01 453 8998 *or* 01 679 5967 (after hours).

Aware: Helping to Defeat Depression
147 Phibsboro Road, Dublin 7. Helpline 01 679 1711.

Childline
c/o ISPCC, 20 Molesworth Street, Dublin 2.
Helpline 1800 666 666.

Irish Hospice Foundation (bereavement support)
64 Waterloo Road, Dublin 4. Tel. 01 660 3111.

Parentline (for parents under stress)
Carmichael House, North Brunswick Street, Dublin 7.
Tel. 01 873 3500.

Samaritans
112 Marlborough Street, Dublin 1. Tel. 01 872 7700
(24 hours a day) *or* Helpline 1850 60 90 90.

Great Britain

Depressive Self-help Group

21 Morningside Gardens, Edinburgh, Scotland E11 10 5LE.

The Manic-depressive Fellowship

13 Rosslyn Road, Twickenham, Middlesex TW1 2AR.
Tel. 0181 892 2811.

Index